EDGAR
ALLAN
POE
at Home

EDGAR ALLAN POE

at Home

CHRISTOPHER P. SEMTNER

THE
History
PRESS

Published by The History Press
Charleston, SC
www.historypress.com

Copyright © 2025 by Christopher P. Semtner
All rights reserved

The images herein are reproduced courtesy of the Edgar Allan Poe Museum,
Richmond, Virginia.

First published 2025

Manufactured in the United States

ISBN 9781467158459

Library of Congress Control Number: 2024949765

This book is dedicated to the memories of friend and Poe Museum supporter Antoinette Suiter and the Poe Museum's beloved cat Pluto.

CONTENTS

INTRODUCTION

I wish there were something to see. Something more than a parking lot, at least. Well, there are some electrical transformers behind the chain-link fence, but nothing remains of Edgar Allan Poe's birthplace. Despite the site being known as where America's most popular author entered this world, the City of Boston saw fit to demolish it in 1959. At least there is a plaque mounted on the adjacent building.

Thanks to my guide, the artist Sandra Luzzi Sneesby, I had picked up a map of Boston Poe sites at a little shop by the Common. The trifold photocopy identified plenty of points of interest, like the place where the theater in which Poe's mother performed once stood or the spot once occupied by the magazine office in which "The Tell-Tale Heart" was first printed, but like his birthplace, those structures were only distant memories.

That leaves me with a bit of a problem. Namely, this is a guidebook to Poe's homes, but there are only four of them left out of the dozens of places he resided in the United States. A few of the lost homes survive in old photos or in the handful of artifacts people managed to salvage from them before the wrecking ball hit, but most are known only through passing mentions in letters or newspaper articles.

There is even less evidence of what went on behind the closed doors of those long-lost houses. The accounts that have somehow survived are often biased, unverifiable or otherwise unreliable. Some of Poe's biographers loved him while others clearly despised him. In this guide, we will cut through a century of myths and legends to catch a glimpse inside Poe's private life and times, which are inseparable from his writing.

Of course, you would not be reading this book if not for Poe's writing. His terror tales have been quickening readers' pulses for nearly two centuries. "The Tell-Tale Heart" reminds us that we cannot escape our conscience. "The Black Cat" asks us to consider what could drive the most gentle and loving man to commit a heinous murder, and "The Cask of Amontillado" is a study in how to enact the perfect revenge. Let's not forget Poe's classic poems like "The Raven," "Annabel Lee" and "The Bells." This guide will transport you back to places and circumstances in which Poe wrote all of these. In the pages to follow, we will search for true cases of grave robbery and murder that inspired Poe's horror tales, the women behind his most famous love poems and the actual bell that inspired "The Bells." Many of these can be found very close to home.

As you join us on this Poe pilgrimage, you will be following in the footsteps of generations of Poe fans, including such literary luminaries as H.P. Lovecraft, who wrote his own brief guide to "Homes and Shrines of Poe" for the Winter 1934 issue of the *Californian*; the Belgian Surrealist painter René Magritte; horror film legend Vincent Price; and countless others who have found inspiration in these Poe places. With that in mind, let us begin our tour of the places Poe did, didn't and might have lived.

Chapter 1

POE'S BIRTHPLACE, BOSTON

*P*oe's mother died a month before his third birthday. He and his infant sister, Rosalie, were present for her final, agonized nights, punctuated by her violent coughing and by the sobbing of the friends and society ladies who had volunteered to tend to her. Eliza Poe, the actress who charmed audiences from Maine to South Carolina, was now alone, abandoned by her husband. To remind herself of happier times, she pulled out a watercolor she had painted of Boston Harbor. On the back, she wrote Edgar a message that he would one day be able to read. It said, "For my little son Edgar, who should ever love Boston, the place of his birth, and where his mother found her best, and most sympathetic friends."

It was in Boston that she launched her career, and it was there that her second son, Edgar, was born on January 19, 1809. Edgar's ill-fated brother, William Henry Leonard Poe, was about three years old. Poe's father, David Poe Jr., almost immediately took off for Pennsylvania to beg for a loan from a wealthy uncle in Pennsylvania named George Poe. According to the latter,

> *One evening he came out to our house—having seen one of our servants....*
> *He had me called out to the door where he told me the most awful moment*
> *of his life was arrived, begged me to come and see him the next day at 11*
> *o'clock at the Mansion house, said he came not to beg, & with a tragedy*
> *stride walked off after I had without reflection promised I would call.*

The next day, when George arrived at the designated meeting place, David was not there. Having gone to a tavern instead, he was apparently unable to attend the meeting and sent a boy to carry a letter pleading for a loan of "30, 20, 15, or even 10$." George did not respond.

Even without a second child, the Poes would have found acting to be a difficult life. Although David and Eliza Poe regularly appeared on the Boston stage, they were struggling to earn a living. Unable to feed her family with David's income alone, Eliza returned to the stage just two weeks after Edgar's birth.

Given what we know about the Poes' finances, their room must have been sparsely decorated with humble furniture. Among their possessions were a miniature portrait of Eliza Poe by her friend, the soon-to-be famous artist Thomas Sully, some sketches, a bundle of letters, a jewelry box, a pocketbook containing locks of the family's hair and Eliza's watercolor of Boston Harbor. There were also a number of scripts and playbills.

The house was probably anything but quiet. Since many of the other rooms in the cramped boardinghouse were occupied by actors from David and Eliza's troupe, the halls surely echoed with the recitation of lines and the rehearsal of songs. Eliza had over two hundred roles to her credit and could be called on at short notice to perform any of about fifty that she knew best. Among her most popular parts was the nine-year-old Little Pickle in the comedy *The Spoiled Child*. The actress had been playing it since she was nine years old, but audiences demanded it of her well into her twenties.

Eliza was also a singer, having debuted on the Boston stage with the song "The Market Lass." Another favorite with her audiences was "Nobody Coming to Marry Me." When fans bought the sheet music, a note printed under the title revealed that this was indeed the song Eliza Poe had performed "to unbounded applause" on the New York stage.

It is unclear how much time David spent rehearsing. Critics complained that he either forgot his lines or tried to rush through them. As indicated by George Poe's account—in addition to an October 10, 1810 New York newspaper notice stating that he would miss that evening's performance "due to a sudden indisposition" (a common euphemism for intoxication)—David had developed a drinking problem. If he was anything like his son Edgar would later become, he could get drunk from a single glass of wine and grow belligerent. In one case, an inebriated David Poe arrived at a theater critic's house in the middle of the night to challenge him over a bad review.

The infant Edgar might have stayed in the Boston house for a little over a month, since a Poe family tradition has it that his parents left him with relatives in Baltimore at the end of February. This may or may not be true. Eliza did not have a long enough break from her performance schedule to make the trip, but David could have left Edgar in Baltimore on his way to meet George Poe near the end of February. Either way, David and Eliza

Taken in 1931, this photograph depicts the boardinghouse in which Poe was born on January 19, 1809. Even though it was known to be Poe's birthplace and was marked with a bronze plaque, the house was demolished in 1959.

This early twentieth-century photograph shows the location of Poe's birthplace. The inscription on the verso reads, "Carver Street, Boston - Looking from Poe Square. Four doors from the corner on the right, stands the house in which Poe was born."

retrieved Edgar from Baltimore in August of that year, during a break between their Boston residence and their time in New York, where they performed from September 1809 until July 1810.

It would be eighteen years before Poe returned to Boston, shortly after running away from home to become a poet. By that time, he could not have remembered anything of his time in the city. In fact, he wrote to a friend in 1835 that he remembered nothing of his parents. All he had was Thomas Sully's miniature of her and the watercolor she made of Boston Harbor.

POE'S BIRTHPLACE AFTER POE

The house in which Poe was born survived well into the twentieth century, but for most of its existence, nobody remembered that Poe had ever lived there. When he died, his obituaries were as likely as not to state that he had been born in Baltimore instead. Over a century later, efforts began in earnest to locate the house by finding the address listed next to David Poe's name in the tax records. They found it at 62 Carver Street, which has since changed its name to Charles Street South. Even better, the house was still standing—and still being used as a boardinghouse.

By 1924, when an article about it appeared in the *Boston Globe*, it was well-known that this was the birthplace of a literary legend. The same year, the Boston Author's Club marked the building with a bronze plaque. The building stood well into the twentieth century, until Boston Edison purchased the property in 1959 and demolished it. Nobody seems to know what happened to the plaque.

It took nearly three decades for the Edgar Allan Poe Memorial Committee, organized by a select group of the nation's Poe scholars and admirers, to place a newer, bigger plaque near the site of Poe's missing birthplace.

VISITING POE'S BIRTHPLACE

You can still visit the site of Poe's birthplace on South Charles Street to see the parking lot. The plaque is located nearby on the side of a building at the corner of Boylston and Charles Streets.

You might be too late to see Poe's birthplace, but you can still find a statue of Poe near the plaque. Designed by Stefanie Rocknak, *Poe Returning to Boston* was installed in the middle of Poe Square in 2014. It depicts an actual-size Poe striding confidently across the sidewalk with his coat trailing behind him as if he were about to take flight. In one hand, he holds a suitcase that has fallen open, allowing a large raven to burst out, spreading its wings. The bronze sculpture proclaims that, over two centuries after his humble birth in a long-lost boardinghouse in that city, he has finally made his triumphant return to Boston.

Chapter 2

POE'S EARLY CHILDHOOD HOMES, RICHMOND

*I*n the late summer of 1811, Eliza Poe arrived in Richmond with Edgar and nine-month-old Rosalie, whose curly black hair and large dark eyes were a near match for her brother's. Henry was gone. Perpetually short on funds, Eliza and David had left him with relatives in Baltimore. Also missing was Edgar's father. A review in the July 26, 1811 issue of the *Norfolk Herald* reported that Eliza was "left alone, the only support of herself and several small children." When he left and where he went are unknown, leading to speculation about Rosalie's paternity. Years later, Poe's foster father wrote that Rosalie was only "half" Edgar's sister.

David last appeared on stage over a year before Rosalie's birth, so he very well could have abandoned his family before her conception. Alternatively, his disappearance from stage could be explained by his being too ill to

Edgar Allan Poe's mother, the actress Eliza Poe, was fifteen and newly married when she sat for this miniature painted by Thomas Sully. After her death, Poe wore the painting in a locket around his neck for the rest of his life.

perform during the last year of his life. As an adult, Edgar wrote that his parents died within a few weeks of each other, and others believed that David succumbed to tuberculosis in Norfolk, Virginia, before Eliza moved to Richmond. If he did, he was likely buried there in an unmarked grave in a potter's field.

Eliza, Edgar and Rosalie took a room in a boardinghouse next to Capitol Square so that Eliza could perform for the season at the Richmond Theater, just across the square. The next few months were a struggle. Even though Eliza's friends helped care for her children, her earnings barely covered the cost of food and rent. The other members of her troupe held benefit performances at which they donated their shares of the admissions to her, but even this proved insufficient when she started missing performances in October.

She was suffering from consumption, a wasting disease that would cause her to deteriorate before young Edgar's eyes. It is unlikely that he understood why she was growing thinner and weaker, drenched in sweat and deathly pale. She struggled to breathe, sometimes choking on her blood, other times coughing up blood mixed with particles of lung tissue.

Consumption, as tuberculosis was then known, was spreading like wildfire throughout the young nation. The growth of cities along the East Coast forced hundreds of thousands into close proximity, squeezing them into cramped rooms in filthy conditions where the highly contagious disease spread through the air with every cough. Every time Eliza coughed, she exposed Edgar and Rosalie to the bacteria that was rotting her lungs. Neither Eliza nor anyone else knew that yet. Before the development of germ theory, even the world's leading physicians had no idea what caused consumption. Some attributed it to miasma (or foul air). Others thought it might be an inherited condition, since it usually afflicted multiple people in the same household. When his three daughters succumbed to the disease, one nineteenth-century Richmonder, Lewis Jahnke, drained his pond, which he blamed for their deaths. A few superstitious people still believed that undead spirits or vampires were at fault. The cure for the latter might be staking the suspected vampires into their coffins or having living sufferers drink the ashes of the recently deceased sprinkled into some wine. The doctor-prescribed remedies were not much better. A trusted physician might administer any number of miracle cures like turpentine, mercury or opium.

It is very likely that tuberculosis bacteria were present in Edgar's lungs for the rest of his life, whether or not he ever manifested any symptoms. For then onward, he would watch, time and again, the disease consume those closest to him without realizing that it was also present in him.

When it was obvious that Eliza was not going to recover, her admirers started to bring her meals. As Richmond merchant Samuel Mordecai wrote to his sister on November 2,

> *A singular fashion prevails here this season—it is—charity—Mrs. Poe, who you know is a very handsome woman, happens to be very sick, and (having quarreled and parted with her husband) is destitute. The most fashionable place of resort, now is—her chamber—and the skill of cooks and nurses is exerted to procure her delicacies.*

When she first came to see Mrs. Poe, one of the visitors, Jane Scott Mackenzie, recalled that the two children appeared "thin and pale and very fretful." With Eliza bedridden, her fellow actor Harriet L'Estrange Usher took care of the children. Mackenzie later related that Usher calmed the anxious children by feeding them bread soaked in gin, a combination that put them right to sleep. She regularly gave them gin and laudanum, a mixture of opium and wine that was used as a painkiller.

One of the other society women caring for Eliza Poe was Frances Valentine Allan, a member of the aristocratic Valentine family and relative of many of the most respected Virginia planters. Having been orphaned herself, she empathized with Edgar's plight, so, after Eliza's death, Allan convinced her husband to take in the future poet.

Mr. Allan, however, was less than enthusiastic about investing in a stranger's child when he was already paying for the education of one of his illegitimate sons. Born in Scotland, John Allan had immigrated to the United States

Robert Matthew Sully painted this portrait of Poe's beloved foster mother, Frances Valentine Allan, shortly before she succumbed to tuberculosis in 1829 at the age of forty-four. Poe had been devoted to her and was deeply offended when her widower remarried the year after her death.

as a young man in search of fortune. He settled in Richmond, where his rich uncle William Galt had already established a successful tobacco export business. In partnership with his friend Charles Ellis, John Allan launched the Ellis and Allan Firm, which also specialized in exporting tobacco.

Eliza Poe passed away on December 8, 1811. Jane Mackenzie's husband, William, convinced the city's only church, St. John's, to allow her remains to be interred there, in an unmarked grave, despite the church's condemnation of her profession.

The artist Thomas Sully, best known for his portrait of Andrew Jackson featured on the twenty-dollar bill, painted this likeness of Poe's foster father, John Allan, around 1804, when the subject was about twenty-five years old and newly married to Frances Valentine.

THE ALLAN HOME, RICHMOND

Having only been Virginia's capital for a few decades, the city of ten thousand retained the feel of a village with antiquated wooden and brick houses dotting the series of hills that stretched along the north bank of the James River. Dominating the landscape from a centrally located hill was the Roman temple that was Thomas Jefferson's Virginia Capitol, the first neoclassical public building in the Americas. In the winter months, when they had time off between the fall harvest and spring plantings on their plantations, the state legislators met there. This is when the sleepy city came to life. The visiting senators and representatives partied and played in what had become known as a raucous and decadent town.

A visitor from Boston was astonished that the sinful Richmonders drank, gambled, danced, went to horse races and attended the theater. Worse still, there was only one poorly attended church for the entire city. Allan fit right into the party atmosphere, developing a taste for heavy drinking and loose women. His marriage did little to curb either of these habits.

About half of the residents were white, and the rest were Black. Of the latter, about two-thirds were enslaved, while one-third were free.

When Edgar entered the Allan household, they put the "Allan" in "Edgar Allan Poe" when they christened him with his new middle name. They were living above John Allan's dry goods store near the corner of Thirteenth and Main Streets. As small as it might have been, the home was bustling with activity. In addition to Edgar and his foster parents, Frances Valentine's adult sister Nancy Moore Valentine lived there. The exact number of enslaved people in the house is not known, but there were probably between one and four. Each would perform multiple tasks. A female slave likely cooked, cleaned, washed and ironed clothes and cared for young Edgar. A male might drive their coach, clean or run errands. Allan also employed a free Black man as his coachman.

One of the few names of enslaved people to be recorded is Judith, who is said to have cared for the three-year-old Edgar. She may be the forty-five-year-old enslaved woman identified as living in the Allan house in the 1810 census. This would make her about forty-six when Edgar arrived. She likely spent more time raising Edgar than his foster parents did. It was she who took him on walks to see his mother's unmarked grave, and she entertained the boy with ghost stories about spirits rising up from their graves to catch little boys. According to Poe's foster uncle Edward Valentine, these tales so terrified the boy that he once bolted in the other direction rather than ride past a cemetery. Poe soon grew to enjoy such folk tales and legends, and he is said to have joined the slaves in the kitchen at night to listen to their stories.

Aside from Judith, there is also documentation of Scipio and Hannah, both of whom Allan hired out after 1815. Another enslaved person there whose name is known is Dabney Dandridge, a coachman who was especially close to the young poet. When the Allans traveled to Virginia's mountain resorts, Poe climbed up onto the top of the coach with Dabney, who wrapped him in a buffalo robe. It took a week or more to reach the hot springs, whose supposedly healing waters were a favorite of the Virginia aristocracy. A favorite spot was White Sulfur Springs, where, judging from the name, the water smelled like rotten eggs—a sure sign at the time that it must have healing properties. Frail and often in ill health, Frances Allan believed the waters could cure her. From the scant evidence that survives, it appears she was suffering from the same disease that claimed Poe's mother. It goes without saying that smelly water would not have provided much relief.

Some of the springs the Allans visited are still open to the public, and a few are resorts. White Sulfur Springs operates to this day under the much more appealing name The Greenbriar.

Back at home, Poe's "solemn beautiful dark gray eyes" worried Frances, who thought he was homesick, so she sent him to play with his sister at Jane Scott Mackenzie's house. After Eliza Poe's death, Jane and William had agreed to take in Rosalie Poe, whom they christened Rosalie Mackenzie Poe.

It was there that Poe made his first lifelong friend. The Mackenzies' oldest son, John Hamilton Mackenzie, was a few years older than Edgar. It was only a couple of weeks after Poe's mother's death, on the day after Christmas, that John was bouncing on a bed and fell, breaking his arm in two places. Jane rushed to his side, canceling her plans to attend the theater that evening. Her sister's sons would go to the play in her place. By the time the doctor finished setting John's arm, Jane's nephews burst through the front door covered in soot. Through faces caked with ash and tears, the boys informed her that the theater was burning. Everyone else in their box was dead, including Jane's best friend Mary Gallego. John's broken arm had saved Jane's life.

Six hundred people had packed into the theater that night to see an evening of entertainment. Midway through the performances, some lit candles on a raised chandelier grazed a canvas backdrop, which became a wick lighting the entire rickety wooden structure. The poor and the Black patrons sitting in the cheap seats downstairs managed to escape, but the wealthy sitting in the exclusive boxes high above the stage were trapped. When they crammed onto the single, narrow staircase, it collapsed under their weight. Some heroes emerged to lower girls out the window, but most of the people upstairs were reduced to unrecognizable heaps of charred meat. The governor's remains were described as a "crisp'd heap." Mary Gallego was only identified by her jewelry, while the embracing skeletons of her foster daughter and the latter's fiancé were identified by his brass buttons.

By the time the sun rose over the smoldering embers that were once a theater, an unknown number of people were injured and seventy-two were dead. It seemed that everyone in town had lost a friend, relative or acquaintance. In addition to the governor, a state senator, the president of the Bank of Virginia and a naval hero had lost their lives. The entire city went into a period of public mourning, and the United States Senate wore black armbands to memorialize the victims of the young nation's first great disaster.

Not long afterward, John was flirting with a little girl when he tumbled down the stairs—breaking his arm again. Apparently, John could not be trusted to stay out of trouble, so Jane Mackenzie decided the best way to

It was in this small bed from the Allan house that the very young Edgar Allan Poe dreamed "dreams no mortal ever dared to dream before." After he outgrew the bed, his foster father, John Allan, gave it to his friend Charles Ellis for his daughter's use. It descended through the Ellis family before entering the Poe Museum's collection.

keep him from injuring himself was to force him to babysit three-year-old Edgar. At first, John tried to entertain the child with fairy tales. Before long, Edgar had turned the tables and was thrilling him with fantastic stories. John later believed this was where Poe first learned to become a storyteller.

Edgar was precocious in other ways. At three, he displayed a talent for performance. The proud Frances showed him off to dinner guests by dressing him in a velvet suit and cape and standing him up on the table to recite poetry.

Frances's cousin Edward Valentine carried the tiny prodigy with him to the store, where Edgar amazed the adults by reading aloud from the newspaper or the works of Shakespeare. Sometimes, Valentine challenged the child to fight other children. The toddler proved himself an able bare-knuckle boxer. Years later, Poe would become one of the best boxers in his academy.

Valentine's bad influence over Poe did not stop there. He also taught Edgar how to pull the chair out from under other boys as they were about to sit down. If making a fool of another kid was funny, Edgar reasoned, humiliating an adult would be hilarious. At one of the Allans' dinner parties, when the gentlemen were holding out chairs for the ladies, he stationed himself behind an especially large woman. A loud thump shook the room, and all the guests turned to see the giggling culprit.

John Allan meted out discipline with a switch. This would prove to be Allan's favorite punishment for the mischievous child's stunts, but it failed to break the boy's spirit. He was soon caught chasing a girl with a toy snake until she cried. An unnamed Allan slave later recounted to Richmond historian Edward Virginius Valentine that Edgar was "a wicked little boy" who had "two heads on him."

Edgar might have had a "wicked" sense of humor, but he was also a sensitive child who enjoyed the company of pets. Frances Allan owned a parrot that could recite the alphabet in French, and Edgar adored a favorite cat named Tib. Over a quarter century later, guests to Poe's homes recalled that he still surrounded himself with cats and birds.

The day after Poe's fifth birthday, John Allan enrolled him in a school run by Clotilda Fisher. Two weeks later, Allan paid for a semester's tuition for one of his illegitimate sons. Fortunately, the two boys were not in the same school.

Outside of the Allan house, the British invaded the United States, taking Washington and burning the White House. Back home, Frances Allan was getting nervous about the war's proximity to Richmond. At one point, the Allans traveled to the mountains when it seemed the British were getting too close to the city. In the end, the War of 1812 spared Richmond, but it devastated the Allans in other ways. Allan's business, the Ellis and Allan Firm, sold American tobacco in England and used the funds to buy European and Asian goods to sell in Virginia. The war with Britain interrupted the shipments, nearly ruining the firm. When peace was finally reached, Allan decided the only way to save the business was to travel to London to establish a British branch of the firm. To that end, Allan sold his furniture, hired out his enslaved workers and took Frances, Nancy and six-year-old Edgar with him across the Atlantic. They never returned to the house on Thirteenth Street.

The young Edgar Allan Poe attended Reverend Bransby's Manor House School in Stoke Newington, London, from 1817 until 1820. He later used it as a setting for his tale "William Wilson" and made an exaggerated version of Bransby one of the characters.

Visiting Poe's First Richmond Home

While nothing near the northwest corner of Ninth and Grace Streets identifies the site of the long-lost actors' boardinghouse, there is an accidental monument directly across Ninth Street in Capitol Square. There, seated on a granite pedestal, is Charles Rudy's bronze statue of Edgar Allan Poe. Completed in 1856, the monument was commissioned by retired physician Dr. George E. Barksdale, who believed that Richmond needed a monument to its misunderstood former citizen. After he donated it to the city, the sculpture sat in storage for two years before the Commonwealth of Virginia could decide where and *if* it should be installed in Capitol Square.

They selected a perfect place, just across the street from the home of Poe's first love Jane Stanard, who inspired his poem "To Helen" before her early death. Since the poem mentions seeing her standing in her window,

The school Poe attended at Stoke Newington, London, was demolished long ago, but this building, which now occupies the site, has been marked with a plaque and a bust of Poe. These serve as reminders that Poe spent five years of his childhood in England. He also stayed briefly with John Allan's relatives in Scotland.

they placed the statue where the bronze figure might glimpse her looking down on him from her window. Rudy's statue sat there until 2017, when the Commonwealth decided to move Poe's monument to make way for a more *important* one.

That is how the Poe statue came to rest on the northwest corner of the square, which unintentionally placed it across the street from Poe's first Richmond home.

VISITING POE'S FIRST HOME WITH THE ALLANS

Just like Poe's birthplace, nothing remains of his first home with the Allans. It was lost in the fire set by evacuating Confederates in the closing days of the Civil War. No photographs or drawings of the house survive, and no plaque marks the spot. Thirteenth Street north of Main is now called Governor's Street, and the northwest corner, where the house once stood, is occupied by the Virginia Retirement System.

BONUS: VISITING POE'S BOARDING SCHOOL IN LONDON

Poe spent three of his five years in London at Reverend Bransby's Manor House school, which became a setting for his tale "William Wilson," which features a character named Dr. Bransby, who is the headmaster of William Wilson's school. The real Bransby, who was still living when the story appeared, was unpleased with his inclusion and remembered Poe as being a spoiled brat.

The school once stood in Stoke Newington, which has since been absorbed by London. Poe pilgrims who cross the pond can find a bronze plaque and a marble bust of Poe on the site at Stoke Newington Church Street, 172.

Chapter 3

FOURTEENTH AND TOBACCO ALLEY, RICHMOND

hen the Allans returned from England, the firm was suffering, and the family moved in with Charles Ellis and his children for about half a year before relocating to a stucco house on Clay Street. After about a year there, the Allans moved to a narrow brick rowhouse sandwiched between Fourteenth Street and Tobacco Alley in the business district. The atmosphere was heavy with the sour aroma of tobacco drying in the warehouse that blocked their view past Fourteenth Street. Poe would have heard drivers shouting at their horses for struggling to pull their carts uphill through the muddy mess that was Fourteenth Street, which wound its way up from the James River on the south to summit of Capitol Hill a few blocks to the north of the Allan house.

The Allans could not have chosen a better location to inspire the budding writer. A short walk to the north was Monumental Church, a memorial to the seventy-two victims of the Richmond Theater Fire of 1811. The screams of the hapless victims, the desperate cries for help that would not come, still echoed in local memories just over a decade later. Edgar and the Allans had only escaped the fire because they were out of town visiting friends on that December night.

The church built over the site of the tragedy was decorated with symbols of death and mourning appropriate to a cemetery because the building was, in fact, the final resting place of those seventy-two unfortunate souls. Naturally, the Allans, who knew several of those victims and their families, owned a pew in the church.

This undated nineteenth-century photograph depicts the home of Charles Ellis, the friend and business partner of Poe's foster father, John Allan. Poe and the Allans lived here for a few months after their return from England in 1820. The house was demolished in 1876.

The bedroom used by Poe's foster mother, Frances Valentine Allan, in Charles Ellis's house is documented in this undated nineteenth-century photograph. Nothing remains of the house, and the block is now occupied by the Richmond Public Library's Main Branch.

Just east of there, on the edge of Shockoe Hill, were the gallows. Thousands had gathered from miles around to witness the public executions there of the rebellious slave Gabriel Prosser in 1800 or of the pirates Galician Felix Barbeto, Jose Morando and Jose Hilario Casaris in 1827. Since the corpses of convicted criminals were fair game for medical schools, the latter three were subjected to galvanic experimentation immediately after they were cut down from the gallows. In such experiments, corpses were given electrical shocks to make their arms, legs, faces and other body parts move. (A similar experiment performed on an Egyptian mummy forms the basis of Poe's tale "Some Words with a Mummy," published almost two decades later.)

Down in that valley was the Shockoe African Cemetery, which housed the remains of countless enslaved people, hastily buried in shallow graves. Foraging dogs and vultures patrolled the grounds, and a little later, grave robbers started harvesting the neglected corpses. The graves were so shallow that a rain heavy enough to make nearby Shockoe Creek flood would cause coffins (and their inhabitants) to float down the business district streets.

These were a grim reminder that something else was being sold in that district besides the tobacco and flour. With the decline of the large Virginia plantations, whose soil had been ruined by two centuries of tobacco and an ignorance of crop rotation, the Deep South's cotton plantations were booming, so Richmond became a center for the sale of the Upper South's slaves to the Deep South. To this end, a complex of slave jails stood about one block east of the Allan house to hold enslaved people in anticipation of the auctions to be held in the hotels along Main Street. There is no evidence that Poe witnessed one of these auctions or saw a group of shackled slaves being led up from the river to the slave jails, but it is difficult to imagine he was not aware of what was happening so close to home. He could likely hear the faint echoes of spirituals sung by enslaved laborers toiling in the nearby warehouses and mills. Literary scholar Killis Campbell believed these songs left their mark on the musicality of the poetry Poe would write decades later.

In contrast to the grim reality of the warehouse district just east of the Allan place, a few blocks west was Court End, the neighborhood surrounding Thomas Jefferson's majestic Virginia Capitol, whose emulation of a Roman temple inspired other Roman and Greek buildings to rise up around the square. This is where the governor and the wealthy judges and lawyers reigned from their grand mansions. During Poe's childhood, Richmond was home to many figures of national prominence, including the Chief Justice of the United States Supreme Court John Marshall, the United States Attorney

Edgar Allan Poe lived in one of the houses at the center of this 1924 photograph from 1822 to 1825. Some researchers believe he occupied the house to the immediate right of the alley while others are convinced he lived in the one to the right of that building. Developers settled the argument by demolishing both of them.

General William Wirt and the distinguished General Winfield Scott. Poe would become acquainted with each of them.

The Allan house was neither as elegant as those mansions nor as cheap as the worst Shockoe Bottom tenements. It was narrow and deep with its wider side facing Tobacco Alley rather than Fourteenth Street. Next to the main house was a kitchen that probably also served as servants' quarters.

It was there that Poe wrote his first poems. Already an avid reader of books from Allan's extensive library, Poe discovered the works of the rebellious British poet Lord Byron, whose poems had gripped the public, making him both famous and infamous. Byron's personality was as prominent as his poems. The archetypical Romantic, he was darkly handsome with wild black curls and a striking profile. Women, and some men, were captivated by him, and he left a trail of broken hearts and shattered lives in his wake. Given his seductive but heartless personality, it is little wonder that his physician John Polidori depicted him as a vampire in the novel *The Vampyre*. Despite a clubbed foot, Byron was athletic, especially when it came to swimming. He famously swam from Greece to Turkey.

The young Poe, who had once pretended to be Robinson Crusoe as he sailed to islands on the James, now struck the Byronic pose by dressing in black, wearing his hair long and wild-looking and sending love poems to the girls in his sister's school. Rosalie dutifully carried them to her classmates for him, and the recipients seemed flattered by his attention—until they realized they had all gotten the same poem. Before long, Dabney was also carrying Poe's love poems to neighborhood girls.

To accomplish a truly Byronic feat, Poe swam six miles against the tide in the James, an accomplishment about which he boasted well into his thirties. By then, so many people thought he was lying that he had some of his childhood friends sign an affidavit swearing that they had seen him do it.

The young Poe also distinguished himself as a boxer, runner, broad jumper and skater. Poe's biographers are uncertain if the latter means ice skating or riding the newly invented roller skates up and down the Allan house halls. He also played bandy, a sport similar to ice hockey.

When he was fourteen, Poe visited his friend, the judge's son Robert Stanard, in his Court End mansion on the western edge of Capitol Square. Into the room walked Rob's mother. Her dark hair, classical features and warm eyes left Poe speechless, unable to breathe. He nearly lost consciousness.

For the next few months, she paid attention to him, provided motherly encouragement and supported his dreams of becoming a poet. Not long after they met, she died, probably claimed by tuberculosis. It was the second time he had lost a mother, and the emptiness drove him to spend the night weeping over her grave at the newly opened Shockoe Hill Cemetery. He would carry the pain with him for the rest of his life, telling women decades later that he loved them because they reminded him of his first love, the one to whom he dedicated the poem "To Helen."

When Poe was living at Tobacco Alley, the Revolutionary War hero Marquis de Lafayette toured the United States to enthusiastic crowds. During his Richmond stop, Poe served on the junior honor guard that escorted him up Main Street, past triumphal arches and ecstatic admirers. For once, Allan could be proud of his ward, but that would not last.

FOURTEENTH AND TOBACCO ALLEY AFTER POE

The Allan House at Fourteenth and Tobacco Alley lasted longer than Poe's other Richmond homes, suffering from decades of neglect before its demolition. Once one of a row of similar buildings, the house was not nearly as much of a landmark as the Allan mansion Moldavia, and historians eventually forgot which building in the row it was. The problem is that John Allan owned two buildings next door to each other, but he lived in only one of them. Insurance records indicate that he lived in the southernmost of the two houses, or 2 North Fourteenth Street, but the question is whether another house had been built south of that house since then. Poe researcher James H. Whitty was convinced that John Allan's house was the one at 4 North Fourteenth Street because it appeared to be of the correct age while the one at 2 North Fourteenth Street had the windows and roofline of a much newer house.

In 1881, Poe's childhood friend Thomas Ellis wrote to Poe's biographer George Edward Woodberry that the Allans had lived in 2 Fourteenth Street and specifically mentioned the tall, thin proportions of the façade, but if this is the Allan house, it is not as wide as the insurance records say it should be.

The confusion continued until the property owners decided to tear down the top floors of 4 Fourteenth Street in 1926. The Poe Museum, which had opened four years earlier, found it impossible to save the house, so the museum's president asked the property owners for the staircase, mantels and anything else that could be saved from the house. These pieces were taken six blocks down the street to be incorporated into the museum's newest addition, the Elizabeth Arnold Poe Memorial Building.

The staircase from Poe's childhood home at Fourteenth Street and Tobacco Alley in Richmond was removed from the house before its demolition and installed in the Poe Museum's newly constructed Elizabeth Arnold Poe Memorial Building, seen here in 1929.

Then the museum made the strange decision to use these materials to build a re-creation of the still-standing building in which they believed Poe's mother had died. Rather than reconstruct the *Allan house* with the pieces of the Allan house, they re-created an entirely different building, which did not need to be reconstructed because it was still standing. If that were not enough, it was soon proven that the house in which they thought Poe's mother had died actually dated to a few years after her death.

In case you have trouble keeping up: the inside of the building was from an Allan house—one that was either Poe's residence or the house next door—but the outside was based on a building that had no connection to Poe. The founders, convinced they got the right Allan house, advertised that their visitors could ascend the very stairs that Poe once strode to his childhood bedroom. The building was then furnished with art and antiques taken from yet another Allan house, Moldavia. A gilded wall sconce, tables, chairs, plates, salt cellars, cut-glass decanters, irons and other Allan possessions filled the first-floor gallery. With none of Poe's homes still standing in Richmond, this was the closest one might get to seeing the environment of his childhood.

VISITING FOURTEENTH AND TOBACCO ALLEY

The houses at Fourteenth and Tobacco Alley are long gone and replaced with a parking deck. Nothing marks the spot. The Allan house stairs and the Elizabeth Arnold Poe Memorial Building can still be visited at the Poe Museum at 1914 East Main Street.

Chapter 4

MOLDAVIA, RICHMOND

Poe was sixteen when everything changed. John Allan's rich uncle William Galt died, leaving him "three landed estates…with the slaves, stocks and property of all kinds belonging thereto." Allan moved from the business district to a huge brick mansion overlooking the James River on the western edge of town. Main Street was unpaved by the time it reached the house, named Moldavia after its first owners, Molly and David Randolph.

Part of the Virginia aristocracy, the Randolphs had been in America for two centuries and counted among their relatives presidents, senators and a Supreme Court chief justice. Theirs was a family of power and influence. In fact, both husband and wife were Randolphs, so Molly had no need to change her last name after their wedding. She was the daughter of a member of the House of Burgesses and the brother of a governor who also happened to be Thomas Jefferson's son-in-law. David was a Revolutionary War officer, and five years before Moldavia's completion, President Washington appointed him the U.S. marshal for Virginia.

After the Randolphs moved into the mansion, Molly established herself as a society hostess. For the next ninety years, Moldavia's halls echoed with balls and dinners attended by the Richmond elite and their distinguished guests. Molly was also the first writer to reside in Moldavia. She is best known as the author of America's first regional cookbook, *The Virginia Housewife*. This popular volume introduced many foreign dishes to American audiences and promoted the use of at least forty different vegetables.

This photograph of Poe's childhood home Moldavia was taken shortly before the mansion's demolition in 1890. Poe's bedroom opened onto the portico on the right, which overlooked the James River, providing unobstructed views for miles up and down the river.

David's career was on the rise until his second cousin Thomas Jefferson's inauguration as president. As a Federalist, Randolph had been a vocal critic of Jefferson, so he lost his job. When Molly and David's fortunes waned, they lost possession of Moldavia and opened a boardinghouse.

With the Virginia aristocrats out of Moldavia, a Spanish-born flour miller named Joseph Gallego took over the mansion. Although some of Richmond's high society were initially skeptical of a member of the merchant class stepping into their world by buying Moldavia, Gallego soon won many friends among them.

He had not lived there long before Gallego lost his wife, his foster daughter and her fiancé in the same Richmond Theater Fire that Jane Scott Mackenzie narrowly avoided. He never recovered from the loss, following them to the grave seven years later, in 1818.

In his will, he left $8,000 to Rosalie Poe's foster mother, Jane Scott Mackenzie, who had been a close friend of his wife and had very nearly joined her at the Richmond Theater that fateful night. He also bequeathed funds for the care of eight-year-old Rosalie. As evidence of the close bond between the Gallegos and the Mackenzies, Jane named one of her children Mary Gallego Mackenzie and another Joseph Gallego Mackenzie. In a portrait of Jane Scott Mackenzie hanging in the Poe Museum, she wears a locket bearing the initials "J.G." for "Joseph Gallego."

Seven years after Gallego's death, John Allan became Moldavia's next owner. Thrust from the verge of bankruptcy to being one of the wealthiest men in Virginia, Allan was determined to show off his fortune and status. Moldavia was the perfect showplace. Passing through the main entrance, guests crossed a parlor to the main dining room, which was octagonal with four walls of floor-to-ceiling windows opposite four of matching floor-to-ceiling mirrors. The room sparkled with cut-glass decanters, salt cellars, glasses and lamps. Showing off that he could afford items from the other side of the earth, Allan purchased a set of intricately glazed eighteenth-century Chinese soup plates. Then he engraved the letter *A* onto his silver and glassware.

The rest of the house was stuffed with European art and antiques, including an Austrian Baroque painting, a set of chairs from a six-hundred-year-old German castle, marble busts, ancient Greek vases and an extensive library—all illuminated by candlelight from ornate gilded wall sconces. Considering the tastes of the time, the walls would have been covered with elaborately patterned wallpaper, and the floors may have been covered with decorative painted oilcloths.

Upstairs were the bedrooms for the Allans, Nancy and Edgar. The latter's room was at the top of a narrow staircase and opened onto the portico that overlooked the James River. Standing there, the young poet could see up and down the river for miles or search the heavens with his telescope, developing a lifelong interest in both astronomy and astrology. For years to come, his poetry would abound with references to planets, stars and constellations and their associated gods and goddesses.

Now that they were living in luxury, Allan took Poe out of

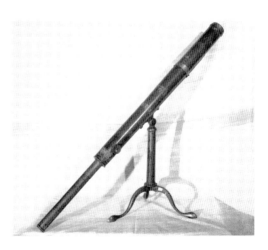

The young Poe studied the stars through this telescope while sitting on the portico of his foster father's mansion perched high above the James River. Poe often references specific stars, planets and constellations in his poetry, and the subject of his last book is the origin of the universe.

the respectable Burke's Academy and enrolled him in the more exclusive school operated by Dr. and Mrs. Ray Thomas near Capitol Square to prepare him for college. If Poe was living like the aristocracy, that didn't necessarily mean they accepted him as one of their own. When the son of an old Virginia family mocked Poe for being a poor orphan and the son of an actress (who probably gave birth to Rosalie out of wedlock), Poe retaliated with an anonymous poem that brutally mocked his rival. Poe distributed "Don Pompioso" among their mutual friends and made sure all the girls in Miss Mackenzie's School read it. Before long, the young aristocrat was a neighborhood laughingstock.

Meanwhile, the schoolgirls started speculating about who the author might be. A few of them were gathered in a parlor around sunset when they handed the manuscript to Poe and asked him to read it to them. They immediately knew he had written it. The room was just dark enough that nobody but the author would have been able to read the poem.

The soon-to-be Master of the Macabre had discovered he had a knack for humorous verse. He followed up "Don Pompioso" with a satire on the members of a debating society and an especially mean-spirited poem mocking a dry-goods store clerk named Robert Pitts who had made the mistake of challenging Poe for a young lady's affections. In the poem, Poe, who was letting John Allan's new wealth go to his head, ridiculed the pretense of someone of Pitt's class associating with upper-class ladies. Poe found humor in the idea that women who are above working for a living could ever fall in love with the mere merchant who sells them ribbon for their shoes. As Poe put it,

> *For at a ball what fair one can escape*
> *The pretty little hand that sold her tape,*
> *Or who so cold, so callous to refuse*
> *The youth who cut the ribbon for her shoes!*

Pitt was so humiliated that he left town. In the end, neither man won the day. She spurned them both and went on to marry a congressman instead.

Poe had become a popular and confident teen known for his wicked sense of humor. He certainly did not lack for camaraderie in the neighborhood. Across the street lived the Mackenzies. Their household included his good friends Tom and John Mackenzie in addition to Poe's sister, Rosalie.

Just up Fifth Street was the home of the merchant James Royster, who had long been a friend and business association of both Allan and William

Galt. Royster had two sons named James and Alexander in addition to an auburn-haired daughter by the name of Elmira. All the boys were captivated by her intelligence and passion. Poe, in particular, was drawn to her talents for poetry and music.

Edgar and Elmira had known each other for years, but their feelings intensified after his move to Moldavia. By this time, they regularly saw each other at parties, where they danced to the fiddle played by a freedman named Old Cy. According to Whitty, who is quoted in Mary Phillips's book *Edgar Allan Poe: The Man*, "She was fond of all the boys, but liked Edgar best, while he was interested in all the girls but lingered longest with Elmira." Poe started showering her with gifts of little pencil sketches of her and likely also addressed poetry to her, none of which has survived. What has remained from their courtship is a tiny mother-of-pearl purse he gave her with their initials engraved on it.

Half a century later, in an interview with Edward Valentine, the transcript of which is housed in the Valentine Museum, she recalled that Poe was "a beautiful boy—Not very talkative. When he did talk though he was pleasant but his general manner was sad." He "hated anything coarse and unrefined [and]…was as warm and zealous in any cause he was interested in, very enthusiastic and impulsive."

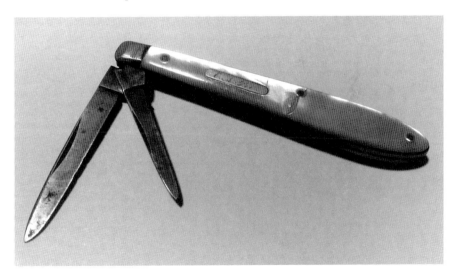

Poe's name is engraved on a little silver plate on the mother-of-pearl handle of his penknife, shown here at the Poe Museum. Although receipts indicate that John Allan bought the young Poe such a knife, this one has not been definitively connected to those documents.

Poe made a point of introducing her to his friends John Hamilton Mackenzie and Ebenezer Burling as well as to his merchant marine brother, Henry, who visited Richmond in 1824 and 1825, staying in Moldavia on the second trip.

For a while, Edgar and Elmira could be seen walking along the canal together or playing duets on her father's piano, but Mr. Royster soon grew concerned about the attention this penniless orphan was paying to his daughter. To continue seeing each other, the young lovers sneaked away to Charles Ellis's walled garden, where they were shielded from her father's disapproving view.

When hiding from her father and his friends, they had to find creative ways to communicate. Legend has it that they signaled each other from their bedroom windows and that Poe recruited Dabney to carry love letters to her.

By the time Poe left for college the following Valentine's Day, they were secretly engaged. He had lived in Richmond for roughly ten of his seventeen years, and he would consider it his home for the rest of his life. Now it was time for him to live on his own for the first time—at the University of Virginia.

Moldavia After Poe

John Allan's second wife, Louisa G. Allan, whom he married after Frances Allan's death, resided in Moldavia for another three decades after Poe's death. The halls resounded with the sounds of the lavish balls for which she earned the reputation as Richmond's leading hostess after Molly Randolph's death. Her three sons—John Allan Jr., Patterson Allan and William Galt Allan—followed in Poe's footsteps by attending the University of Virginia. Their mother rewarded them after graduation by taking them on a five-year grand tour of Europe.

Shortly after their return, the Civil War broke out, and the three Allan boys joined the Confederate army. Back on the homefront, entrenched soldiers surrounded Richmond to defend the Confederate capital. Both Poe's sister and his friend Susan Talley witnessed their yards scarred with trenches and their trees cleared for battle. Rosalie Poe fled for the North to stay with family in Baltimore while Susan Talley took a different route— she became a Confederate spy. After being captured and imprisoned, she fell in love with a Union officer. She married him and had a son before divorcing him.

In Moldavia, Louisa rolled bandages for the countless wounded soldiers arriving daily from the surrounding battlefields. While Patterson and his brothers were fighting for the Confederacy, his wife was arrested for spying on behalf of the Union. She was one of an unknown number of Richmonders secretly working for the North. Among them was Poe's friend Elizabeth Van Lew, who, in her mansion a block west of Elmira's house, hid escaped slaves headed north as well as Union officers breaking out of Libby Prison—all with the unwitting superintendent of Libby Prison boarding under her roof.

John Allan Jr. fell two days after the Battle of Gettysburg, and his brother William Galt Allan returned home to marry his widow, only to die three years after the war's end. The final Allan son lived only another seven years after returning from the war. Louisa outlived all three of her children by over a decade. After her passing in 1881, her executors auctioned off the items remaining in the mansion. These included paintings, antique furniture,

Poe's foster parents once entertained distinguished guests in this parlor, but by the time Richmond photographer George Cook took this picture of Poe's childhood home Moldavia in 1885, Lily Logan was teaching art classes there. This is the only known interior photograph of the Allan mansion.

glassware, sculpture and just about everything else that was not nailed down. A few items, like a doorbell and a gilded sconce, had to pried off the walls since, by this time, Poe's notoriety was such that almost everyone in town clamored for something—anything—from his childhood home.

In the years that followed, various renters took over the property. As a child, the mother of Richmond architectural preservationist Mary Wingfield Scott lived upstairs. Knowing of Poe's association with the house, she imagined that the mysterious footsteps she heard ascending the stairs at night were those of Poe's ghost. Or maybe, she reconsidered, they were mice.

In 1884, the sixtieth anniversary of Lafayette's visit to Richmond, a committee decorated Moldavia for its last great ball. The following year, the artist Lily Logan rented the rapidly deteriorating structure to teach art classes in the parlor in which the Allans had entertained their guests a half-century earlier.

By 1890, the mansion was crumbling. Photos from the time show broken windows and an overgrown yard. That year, the new owners tore down the house and replaced it with a row of commercial buildings.

VISITING THE MOLDAVIA SITE

In 1906, the Association for the Preservation of Virginia Antiquities installed a plaque on the Fifth Street wall of one of the unremarkable storefronts that had replaced Moldavia. As of the time of this writing, the plaque is still visible, but it is not on the exact spot. To stand in the footprint of the lost Moldavia, walk around to the back of the building and stand in the middle of the small parking lot. You will be at just about the location of the mansion's main entrance facing Fifth Street.

Although the house is no more, you can still see several of the Allans' furnishings fifteen blocks down Main Street at the Poe Museum. There you can find several of their chairs, tables, china, glassware, silverware—and even one of their gilded wall sconces. Many of these items trace their provenance directly back to Louisa Allan's estate sale. Some of the other Moldavia pieces found their way to the Enoch Pratt Free Library, which you will be visiting on your Poe pilgrimage to Baltimore.

VISITING THE ELLIS GARDEN

The site of the Ellis House on the southwest corner of Second and East Main Streets is now occupied by the Main Branch of the Richmond Public Library, but their walled garden across Main Street is a site worth visiting on your Poe pilgrimage. Where once stood the Ellis garden in which Poe used to sneak away to see Elmira Royster, there is now a series of old row houses that have been converted into the Linden Row Inn. If you decide to spend the night in Richmond, stay in their Poe Suite decorated with Poe portraits. Then explore their courtyard, which is about all that remains of the Ellis garden. Their resident cat Annabel patrols the courtyard and greets guests. There is even a legend that Poe's mother's ghost haunts the place, but I don't believe it. She never had any association with the garden or any of the buildings on that block.

Chapter 5

POE'S DORM ROOM,
UNIVERSITY OF VIRGINIA

oe arrived at Jefferson's new University of Virginia on Valentine's Day 1826. From his early days, Poe preferred to sit atop the carriage, wrapped up in an old buffalo robe, next to Allan's enslaved carriage driver, so he was likely perched up there to witness the first glimpses of this educational experiment. The overland journey from Richmond to the low, rolling mountains of Charlottesville had taken the better part of a week before the carriage finally trudged through the last few muddy miles to arrive at Jefferson's Rotunda, its unfinished dome rising above the treetops. Extending behind the structure was the Lawn, flanked by long, low buildings extending like arms from the Rotunda. Allan dropped off Edgar with roughly $110 to pay his expenses and headed back to Richmond.

Although he had missed the first day of classes by two weeks, Poe was one of five students to arrive that day. He was the 136th of 177 students to register that year, the second of the school's existence. He could hear the construction going on overhead and see crates of books being hauled to the library. What he did not see was the chapel, which should have held the central location occupied by the Rotunda. Unlike the new nation's other major colleges and universities, this was to be a nonsectarian institution. The founder, Thomas Jefferson, was, after all, the author of the Virginia Statute of Religious Freedom, and he envisioned his university as an enlightened environment promoting free thinking and preparing students for public service. Students were extended the freedoms of self-government and the ability to choose their own curricula. Opposed (at least in principle) to the institution of slavery, Jefferson forbade students from bringing slaves with them to campus. This stood in contrast to other southern universities like William and Mary, which required students to bring their own slaves. The students, mainly the sons of wealthy planters, circumvented the rules by hiring slaves from nearby tavern owners to clean their rooms and wash their clothes.

Since Jefferson's school was the most expensive in the country, Poe could register for only two of the expected three courses for his first term. This cost $60, leaving him $50 for board, at a cost of $110. To this he added $15 for his room, $12 for a bed and $12 for furniture. Because this did not include the cost of books or other supplies, Poe wrote to Allan a couple of weeks later to request more money and a French textbook. Allan chided him in response and sent Poe a mathematics book even though the poet could not afford to attend any math classes. He had opted to study ancient and modern languages, a degree the businessman Allan apparently considered useless. The math book was likely a hint that Poe should focus on classes that would prepare him to take over Allan's export business. That left Poe to borrow from local money lenders at high interest rates.

He moved into a room in the center of everything on the West Lawn. His front door opened into a green courtyard with the Rotunda to his left.

Poe lived here on the West Range while attending the University of Virginia. In 1826, he witnessed one classmate biting another man just outside of his front door, which was under the eighth arch from the left. The photograph was taken in 1926 by Hervey Allen.

How long he stayed there is uncertain, but it could not have been more than four months. By then, he had gotten into a brawl with his roommate and moved to "Rowdy Row," on the West Range. His room was either 13 or 17 West Range, but in the absence of conclusive evidence, the school has since designated 13 the Poe Room. Thirteen sounds creepier than seventeen anyway.

Whichever number it was, his new room faced away from the Lawn and toward the Anatomy Theater across the street. A student of the Enlightenment, Jefferson believed from its inception that his school should host gross anatomy lectures fully stocked with fresh cadavers. One of the first eight faculty members he hired was a professor of medicine and anatomy. Jefferson himself designed the two-story brick anatomy hall. The first floor was a museum featuring displays of skeletons and medical oddities. The top floor was the theater in which the dissections took place. The basement was where the bodies were stored and prepared.

Students in Poe's time complained about the stench of rotting human flesh wafting across the street to the West Range. The summer heat, accelerating the rate of decay, made the odor especially unbearable. It got so bad that, in 1833, the University finally constructed a small building next door for the immediate boiling of dissected cadavers. Of course this was well after Poe left the school.

During his time, he might also have witnessed the discreet delivery of oblong boxes to that brick building across the street from his dorm room. Since the school needed cadavers, it was obliged to find a way to procure them. With the state not providing enough subjects, the faculty and students took it upon themselves to venture to local cemeteries under the cover of darkness to locate freshly dug graves. While northern universities procured bodies of the poor from potter's fields, southern schools preferred to raid slave and freedmen cemeteries and to use slaves to do the dirty work. The name of the slave the University of Virginia enlisted to find cadavers has been lost to time, but his successor, hired out from a local landowner and known as Anatomy Lewis, served in that capacity for nearly two decades.

When the supply of local bodies ran dry, the University ordered some of the ones being stolen for the same purpose from the slave cemetery in Richmond by the Medical College of Virginia's resident grave robber. How much Poe *saw* of the grisly work performed across the street from his dorm room is unknown, but he surely *smelled* it.

It would almost a decade before grave robbing and the dissection of cadavers started to show up in Poe's writing when he created tales like "The

Loss of Breath," "Berenice" and "The Fall of the House of Usher." In the latter, Roderick Usher hides his sister's coffin in his basement rather than bury it in the family cemetery because he is worried that her doctors will steal her body.

In the meantime, Poe's letters home to the Allans reveal an interest in the violence and gore he encountered just outside his front door. On May 25, 1826, he wrote to Allan that the school was so violent that "a common fight is so trifling an occurrence that no notice is taken of it." Poe continued by recounting how a student had struck another in the head with a rock, only to have the victim pull a pistol on him. Luckily, the pistol misfired.

In the same letter, Poe tells Allan about the fifty students who spent the day hiding in the woods to avoid being arrested by the sheriff for rioting. That month, Poe's classmates Thomas Barclay, James Albert Clarke and J. Armistead Carter were suspended. Another student, Sterling Edmunds, was suspended for horsewhipping a boy who had beaten him at cards.

When this photograph of the interior of Poe's University of Virginia dorm room was taken by Hervey Allen in 1926, the furniture and mantel were far nicer than they had been in Poe's day. Poe's furniture no longer exists because he broke it down for firewood to heat the room.

In a September 21 letter, Poe informed Allan,

> *We have had a great many fights up here lately—The faculty expelled*
> *Wickliffe last night for general bad conduct—but more especially for biting*
> *one of the student's arms with whom he was fighting—I saw the whole*
> *affair—it took place before my door—Wickliffe was much the strongest*
> *but not content with that—after getting the other completely in his power,*
> *he began to bite—I saw the arm afterwards—and it was really a serious*
> *matter—It was bitten from the shoulder to the elbow.—and it is likely that*
> *pieces of flesh as large as my hand will be obliged to be cut out.*

It would appear that Poe did not need to look far to find the gruesome and disturbing subject matter that would become the hallmarks of his mature short stories. He just didn't know it yet. The tale he chose to share with his classmates that semester was a long and amusing comedy about a man named Gaffy. His friend Thomas Goode Tucker later recalled that the piece was "entirely free from his usual sombre coloring and sad conclusions merged in a mist of impenetrable gloom." When Poe's friends dared ridicule the work, he hurled the manuscript into the fire. Thereafter, they taunted him with the appellation Gaffy Poe.

Despite this early disappointment, Poe spent another decade writing comedies and romances before he published his first horror story, "Berenice," which just happens to include both the stench of decaying flesh and grave robbery. About the same time, Poe wrote "Loss of Breath," a comedy about a man who, mistaken for dead, is sold to an anatomist who begins to dissect him. Without realizing it, Poe had already found the subject matter he needed to revolutionize the horror genre, but it would take several more years of writing comedies to incorporate grave robbery, decaying corpses and graphic violence into his fiction.

While Poe was making some initial efforts in prose, he was still obsessed with poetry, and his classmates recalled him reciting passages from favorite poems in solemn tones. (No doubt, he was the life of the party.) He also connected with other student writers by joining the Jefferson Literary Society, which elected him its secretary.

While his comrades acknowledged his talent for poetry, they thought he might just become a painter instead of a poet. As evidence, they cited the strange and grotesque drawings he executed in charcoal on his dorm room's plaster walls. Poe also became fascinated with a book of British artist William Hogarth's satirical engravings. The penniless student could not afford to buy

While attending the University of Virginia, Poe studied, completed his homework and composed poetry on this lap desk, which is now on display at the Poe House and Museum in Baltimore.

the book, so he and his friend pooled their money to buy it. When Poe tired of sharing it, he rolled dice to see who would keep it. Poe lost the bet and found himself paying for someone else's book.

Otherwise, Poe's classmates described him as an exceptional athlete and student, but according to his friend Thomas Bolling, "My impression was and is that no one could say that he knew him—He wore...a sad, melancholy face always, and even a smile, for I don't remember his ever having laughed heartily, seemed to be forced."

It seemed that Poe was hiding some deep sorrow. Maybe it was the fact that Elmira Royster had yet to answer any of his letters. At the same time, the stress of his growing debts was weighing him down. By the end of his first year, he had started breaking apart his furniture to make firewood to heat his room. He had never been able to afford the textbook for his French course, so he passed his class by borrowing a classmate's book before class to memorize each day's lesson. Against all odds, he managed to finish the year as one of the top four French students.

To escape the pressures of school and his anxiety over Elmira's silence, he fled to the nearby Ragged Mountains, where he roamed through unspoiled wilderness still populated by cougars, wolves and bears. His short story "A Tale of the Ragged Mountains" provides a description of what he found (or at least wanted to find) there:

> *It was about nine in the morning when I left Charlottesville. I bent my steps immediately to the mountains, and, about ten, entered a gorge which was entirely new to me. I followed the windings of this pass with much interest.—The scenery which presented itself on all sides, although scarcely entitled to be called grand, had about it an indescribable, and to me, a delicious aspect of dreary desolation. The solitude seemed absolutely virgin. I could not help believing that the green sods and the gray rocks upon which I trod, had been trodden never before by the foot of a human being. So entirely secluded, and in fact inaccessible, except through a series of accidents, is the entrance of the ravine, that it is by no means impossible that I was indeed the first adventurer—the very first and sole adventurer who had ever penetrated its recesses.*

Poe's other method for calming his anxiety was drinking. The only problem is that he could not handle his alcohol. A single glass incapacitated him. As his friend Tucker recalled,

> *Poe's passion for strong drink was as marked and as peculiar as that for cards. It was not the taste of the beverage that influenced him; without a sip or smack of the mouth he would seize a full glass, without water or sugar, and send it home at a single gulp. This frequently used him up; but if not, he rarely returned to the charge.*

Poe's comrade Upton Beall invited him to play cards and plied him with glasses of peach and honey scooped from a punch bowl until Poe lost all the money he had left—and much more. By the end of the year, Poe had racked up at least $2,000 in gambling debt. With paying his current tuition and fees out of reach, returning for another year was impossible, but somehow he continued to excel in his studies.

A few months into Poe's first semester, the school library opened. Poe started frequenting the stacks in search of French history books. In quick succession, he borrowed *Histoire Romaine* by Charles Rollin, *The History of America* by William Robertson, *The Life of George Washington* by John Marshall, two volumes of Voltaire's works and *Nature Displayed in Her Mode of Teaching Language to Man, Or A New and Infallible Method of Acquiring a Language, In the Shortest Time Possible, Deduced from the Analysis of the Human Mind, and Consequently Suited to Every Capacity* by Nicolas Gouïn Dufief. He checked out the last one, a guide for rapidly learning languages, about a month before his final examination in ancient and modern languages. Most of the other books consisted of histories and biographies. Throughout his writing career, Poe drew on historical events and legends to inspire his tales and poems, many of which are set long ago in distant lands.

Two of the books were the works of the French humorist, philosopher and author Voltaire. These were either volumes of his letters or of his complete works. One imagines that Voltaire's humor appealed to Poe, who still fancied himself a humorist.

That summer, at Thomas Jefferson's nearby plantation Monticello, the former president, author of the Declaration of Independence and founder of the University of Virginia breathed his last. It was July 4, 1826, the fiftieth anniversary of his Declaration. By coincidence, he and the nation's second president, John Adams, died within hours of each other.

When news of Jefferson's passing reached Charlottesville, the townspeople, students and faculty started fighting over who would lead the procession to his funeral at Monticello. On the chosen day, over one thousand people jockeyed for a place at the front of the line, causing such a delay that they arrived late for the service. Unable to wait any longer, the president's family decided to start the funeral without them. A witness recalled seeing Poe, who apparently chose to walk to Monticello on his own without waiting for the rest of his class.

At the end of the year, an informant implicated Poe as one of nine students who were aware that local tavern keepers had been drinking and playing cards with students in their dorm rooms. The faculty brought Poe to testify before them about his involvement in these illegal activities. While he is known to have lost thousands in games of chance and certainly could have played cards with the tavern keepers, Poe declared that he had no knowledge of any infractions.

The next day, Poe headed to Richmond for the Christmas break. Despite being among the top students in the school of ancient and modern languages, he would never return. Allan paid some of his debts and put the poet to work without pay in the Ellis and Allan counting rooms in the hopes that Poe would at least learn one useful skill—bookkeeping—since college, in Allan's opinion, had been only a waste of time and money.

Poe summed up the experience fifteen years later when he wrote to the editor Rufus Griswold,

> *In 1825 [I] went to the Jefferson University at Charlottesville, Va., where for 3 years I led a very dissipated life—the college at that period being shamefully dissolute. Dr. Dunglison of Philadelphia, President. Took the first honors, however, and came home greatly in debt. Mr. A. refused to pay some of the debts of honor, and I ran away from home without a dollar on a quixotic expedition to join the Greeks, then struggling for liberty.*

The truth is that Poe had matriculated in 1826 and stayed just under one year. Rather than earning "first honors," he dropped out. The story about trying to join the Greek Wars of Independence was also entirely fabricated. Otherwise, there is some truth to the story.

Poe's year at the University partially inspired his tale "William Wilson." After leaving Bransby's school, the vile title character attends Oxford, "the most dissolute university of Europe," and clearly a stand-in for Poe's University of Virginia. Reminiscent of Poe's own experience, Wilson is a drinker and gambler.

POE'S DORM ROOM AFTER POE

Over the years, numerous other students stayed in Poe's dorm room. The walls were replastered and repainted multiple times, and the room was redecorated and updated. The university expanded beyond its initial footprint with buildings rising in all directions around the Rotunda.

The University eventually demolished the old Anatomy Theater, that reminder of one of the darkest chapters in the school's history, but like the dead in a Poe story, the past did not stay buried forever. Excavations of the grounds in front of the Alderman Library in 1997 uncovered the discarded bones of some of those unfortunates who were dissected there.

It was about four decades after Poe's death that Charles Kent, the University's professor of English literature, started the movement to honor the University's most famous dropout. By this time, French intellectuals revered Poe as a groundbreaking and influential author, but the fashion among American university professors was to dismiss Poe as merely a popular writer of trashy stories. Kent, however, bucked the trend by calling attention to Poe's contributions and defending his reputation as an author and a man.

In 1897, Kent wrote an article for the campus paper calling for Poe's room to be converted into a museum of Poe memorabilia. In the spring of that year, Kent convened a mass meeting of students to establish a Poe Memorial Association, which soon commissioned the Hungarian-American sculptor George Julian Zolnay to sculpt a bronze bust of Poe to be unveiled on the fiftieth anniversary of the poet's death. In fact, the year 1899 was correct, but they unveiled it on Poe's birthday (January 19) instead of on the day of his death (October 7). The bust is now on display in the Alderman Library, where it can often be seen wearing a UVA sweatshirt.

In 1904, a student named William McCully James suggested to the faculty that they establish an honor society as an alternative to the University's more exclusive literary and social clubs. The faculty selected twelve of the best students to draw up a constitution for the new organization. It took a little over a week for the students to elect a chairman and establish the group's goal to "bring together the best men in the various departments of the University for mutual acquaintance and for cooperation in their efforts to protect the honor and dignity of the University."

When the time came to name this society, the members proposed and rejected a succession of ideas before someone called it the Raven Society, in reference to Poe's most famous poem. Two years later, the University's President and Board of Visitors charged the Raven Society with maintaining Poe's dorm room.

By this time, the school had decided that 13 West Range would be the Poe Room. Whether or not it is the correct one, that has been the Poe Room ever since.

In 1924, Professor Edmund S. Campbell of the University's School of Architecture refurnished the room in a style appropriate to Poe's time. A quarter century later, the University remodeled additions made after 1826, including that marble mantel. At the same time, a descendant of Allan's business partner Charles Ellis provided Poe's actual childhood bed for the room. That bed, of course, is now in the Poe Museum and has been replaced with one of the style used in the University's dorms in 1826.

While Poe has yet to receive a posthumous degree from the University, one of its librarians, Harry Clemons, finally paid Poe's library fines over a century too late.

VISITING POE'S DORM ROOM

Today's Poe pilgrims can find the Poe Room off McCormick Road near the large Edgar Allan Poe historical marker. The door is covered with glass to allow a peek inside at the simple furnishings consisting of a table, a couple of chairs, copies of the books Poe read while living there and a bed covered in a period-appropriate coverlet. A suit of clothes of the kind Poe would have worn has been laid across the bed as if Poe just stepped out of the room for a second. Pressing a button on the door frame plays a recording about Poe's year at the University.

A short walk to the right of the Poe Room brings you to the room used by the Jefferson Debating Society, the group for which Poe served as the secretary. Each Halloween, the members host a Poe reading contest in which students compete to deliver the most effective performance of a Poe poem, tale or essay. After judging the contest one year, a member of the Raven Society invited me to step inside the Poe Room and sit in the chair. While the room is not huge, it feels larger inside than it seems from the outside. It is easy to imagine Poe spending his evenings there, hunched over a pile of history books, writing his infamous "Gaffy" story. Standing on the threshold, looking out toward McCormick Road, one can envision Poe on that very spot, watching his classmate bite a man right there in front of him.

Poe pilgrims will also want to visit the nearby Rotunda to see a pane of glass taken from Poe's dorm room window. Someone scratched into the pane,

> *O Thou timid one, let not thy*
> *Form rest in slumber within these*
> *Unhallowed walls,*
> *For herein lies*
> *The ghost of an awful crime.*

Legend has it that Poe composed those verses during his brief but tumultuous residence in that room, but this is unlikely. If you would like to see some actual Poe artifacts, make an appointment to see the Poe manuscripts in the Small Special Collections Library across the street from Poe's dorm room. Afterward, head to the school bookstore to buy a T-shirt bearing a Poe portrait beneath the UVA logo and above the words "Distinguished Dropout."

Chapter 6

FORT INDEPENDENCE, MASSACHUSETTS

*I*t must have been a long carriage ride home to Richmond. Five days sitting next to his foster father would have been awkward enough for the young poet, but *this* ride must have been unbearable. Allan had paid off all of what he considered Poe's legitimate college debts, but he would not touch the thousands of dollars Poe lost at the card table. One hopes that Poe was able to escape by climbing up top to sit next to Dabney.

When they finally reached Richmond, Poe was anxious to see Elmira. Although he had sent her letters from Charlottesville, it had been months since he had received anything from her. Then he learned the truth. Exactly how this happened is a matter of debate. According to one account, Poe rushed from Moldavia to Elmira's house only to find himself at a party to which he had not been invited. His heart sank when he saw Elmira on the arm of her fiancé, Alexander Barrett Shelton, the wealthy and handsome owner of a shipping business on the canal. Only later did Poe and Elmira discover that her father had intercepted their love letters to convince her to break off the engagement.

Another, less dramatic version, says that Elmira was out of town visiting relatives when Poe returned from the university and that he found out about her engagement from Dabney or a friend. Either way, the result was the same.

After an especially violent argument with his foster father, Poe stormed out of Moldavia. The recent college dropout had been working off his debts in John Allan's office but could no longer bear living under Allan's roof.

Poe's decision was a bit rash. The next day he wrote to Allan for assistance because he had forgotten to bring any money or clothes with him when he ran away from home. He wrote to Allan, pleading for his trunk and some cash, but received no response. Eventually, Poe and Ebeneezer Burling stowed away on a northbound coal ship. Burling lost his nerve and hopped off the ship at Norfolk. Poe sent word home with him that he was headed for Europe to join the Greek War of Independence. For the rest of his life, Poe repeated the story of his European sojourn, how he was captured and imprisoned in Russia and how he traveled to England after the U.S. minister to Russia secured his release. These accounts appeared in articles about him during his lifetime and for years after his death. People claimed to have met him in Europe, and there was supposedly a portrait painted of him in London. The famous French author Alexandre Dumas even wrote about meeting Poe in Paris.

Of course, Poe made up the whole thing. The painting and the Dumas account, the manuscript of which is housed in the Free Library of Philadelphia, are both fakes. The truth is much more mundane. Poe visited relatives in Baltimore before moving to Boston to launch his literary career. It is difficult to trace Poe's movements during the next few months. He may have tried his hand at acting. He almost certainly worked as a clerk.

When his friend from the university Peter Pindar Pease ran into him in Boston, Poe begged Pease not to tell anyone where he was or what had become of him. He related to Pease that he had worked as a clerk for two months but was not paid all the money due him. Then Poe found employment reporting for a paper that immediately went out of business. When Poe's landlady evicted him, he decided to join the army.

On May 26, 1827, the eighteen-year-old poet went to Castle Island and enlisted in the U.S. Army for five years. He gave his name as Edgar A. Perry; his birthplace, Boston; his profession, "clerk;" his eye color, gray; his hair color, brown; his height, five feet, eight inches; and his age, twenty-two. Poe lied about his age because he was too young to enlist without his guardian's permission. He had other reasons for using an assumed name. Creditors from Charlottesville had followed him back to Richmond to demand payment. This was one of the reasons he had quarreled with Allan and left town in the first place. It is also likely why he asked Pease not to tell anyone he was in Boston.

This did not mean he had given up on his literary aspirations. Poe convinced a Boston job printer named Calvin Thomas to print a small collection of his poems. Forty pages long and about the size of an almanac,

Tamerlane and Other Poems contains a single long poem and nine short ones. The title poem concerns the real-life Turco-Mongol military leader Timur, who conquered much of Asia while cultivating the arts and architecture. Before Poe's time, Timur, also known as Tamerlane, Tamburlaine and Timour, was the subject of plays by Christopher Marlowe, Nicholas Rowe, Matthew Lewis and others in addition to operas by George Frideric Handel, Antonio Vivaldi and Josef Mysliveček. Poe used the character as his narrator, but instead of focusing on Timur's conquests (or even his tendency to erect pyramids out of the skulls of the vanquished), Poe relates an apocryphal tale of the young Timur falling in love with a girl named Ada. When Timur is possessed by a desire for power and glory, he abandons her to conquer the world. In later years, he returns to discover that she has died in his absence and that none of his worldly success means anything without her at his side. It is easy to interpret this as a thinly veiled retelling of his engagement to Elmira, who broke up with him while he was at the University of Virginia.

A short poem in the collection called "Song" describes a bride on her wedding day. As she walks down the aisle, she is filled with shame for marrying the wrong man. This, too, could relate to his failed relationship.

Overall, the collection's quality is uneven, and the text suffers from typographical errors and bad printing. He disliked some of the verses so much that he never reprinted them in his later books, but a few of the poems—early versions of "The Lake," "Spirits of the Dead" and "A Dream Within a Dream"—show promise and hint at what would lie ahead for the writer. Unfortunately, nobody seems to have noticed. It attracted no critical attention and didn't sell.

Thomas could have printed as many as two hundred copies or as few as forty. Either way, Poe never paid for the books or owned a copy. By the time of his death, there were no known copies, so most people thought he had lied about having written the book. Since then, only twelve copies have been located.

Poe reported to duty at Fort Independence on Castle Island, across Boston Harbor from the city. The massive granite walls formed a pentagon with parade grounds in the center. The east-facing wall of the pentagon was the barracks for enlisted men, where Poe stayed during his time there. From between the cannons lined up along the top of the fort, he could peer out across the harbor he had grown up seeing in his mother's watercolor.

Nearby stood the monument to Lieutenant Robert F. Massie, a popular and beloved soldier who had died there in a duel with Lieutenant Gustavus

Drane on Christmas Day, exactly ten years earlier. Rumors spread about Drane's sudden disappearance afterward. It was whispered that Massie's friends had avenged his death by bricking up Drane alive behind a wall. This is exactly the kind of story that would have intrigued Poe. Characters get buried alive throughout his tales, most notably in "The Cask of Amontillado." Poe might very well have heard the legend, but that didn't make it true. The real Drane's corpse was not hidden within Fort Independence's walls. He wasn't even dead. Not only was he still alive, but he continued to serve in the military until 1846 as well.

Another Castle Island legend has it that construction workers were tearing down a wall in 1905 when they uncovered a skeleton that appeared to be dressed in the decayed remnants of an old army uniform. Judging from his position, which indicated a struggle, he had been put behind the wall when he was still alive. Nobody seems to know who he might have been—or if the story is true.

When he was assigned to Battery H of the First Artillery at Fort Independence, Poe probably felt acutely out place among the twenty-eight other privates in his fifty-man battery. After all, university-educated gentlemen of Poe's time usually became officers. In fact, being an officer could elevate a merchant to the status of gentleman. It is unsurprising that Poe had more in common with his officers than with his fellow soldiers, and some of these officers had served alongside Poe's paternal grandfather, "General" David Poe, and took a personal interest in the younger Poe's well-being.

His fellow enlisted men were typically immigrants or the poor, or those a contemporary British visitor to the United States, whose comments are recorded in William Hecker's *Private Perry and Mister Poe*, referred to as "the scum of the population" and "the worthless German, English, or Irish emigrants." When they enlisted, these outcasts were tasked with backbreaking manual labor, including building roads, constructing fortifications, cutting firewood and manning cannons. It took five men to fire a cannon, and chances of being killed or injured by the recoil or an explosion were high. Poe was fortunate that his commanding officers knew him well enough to spare him from those duties by assigning him to be the company clerk. His education and his unpaid position in John Allan's counting rooms had overqualified him for the job, but the steady pay of five dollars per week, while far from great, helped save him from destitution.

His work consisted of drafting correspondence for officers, preparing payrolls, and serving as a messenger. These tasks excused him from manual labor and guard duty, but this likely further distanced him from the soldiers with whom he lived in the barracks.

For the time being, army life satisfied Poe, but he wanted more. Memories of his grandfather's service in the Revolutionary War, his hero Lord Byron's attempt to join the Greek War of Independence and Poe's own role on Lafayette's honor guard might had stirred up his patriotic spirit. But he had joined the army during a prolonged period of peace, so his battery never got called into combat.

VISITING FORT INDEPENDENCE

When you are in Boston to visit Poe's birthplace, you should head over to Castle Island to see where Poe was stationed during the first months of his military career. Fort Independence closed long ago, but you can still walk around the fort's exterior. By the way, Castle Island is no longer an island but a peninsula because it was connected to the mainland in 1928. While there, you can explore the walking trails, watch planes take off from Logan Airport and partake of some fried seafood. Don't bother looking for Lieutenant Robert F. Massie. His body was exhumed and moved off-site during World War II.

From downtown Boston, Poe pilgrims can reach Castle Island by subway on the red line, and the 7, 9, 10 and 11 buses also have stops near there. Another option is to take a ferry.

Chapter 7

FORT MOULTRIE, SOUTH CAROLINA

oe was only stationed at Fort Independence for half a year before the army ordered his battery to Fort Moultrie, across the bay from Charleston. It took eleven days over stormy seas and driven snow for the brig *Waltham* to carry them down the coast to South Carolina.

The vast sandy beaches that greeted him on Sullivan's Island could not have been more different than Boston. Back there the leaves had fallen, but here the palmettos and myrtles were still lush and green. Much of the island was still wild and unspoiled.

In Poe's tale "The Gold-Bug," his narrator gives his impressions of Sullivan's Island:

> *This Island is a very singular one. It consists of little else than the sea sand, and is about three miles long. Its breadth at no point exceeds a quarter of a mile. It is separated from the main land by a scarcely perceptible creek, oozing its way through a wilderness of reeds and slime, a favorite resort of the marsh-hen. The vegetation, as might be supposed, is scant, or at least dwarfish. No trees of any magnitude are to be seen. Near the western extremity, where Fort Moultrie stands, and where are some miserable frame buildings, tenanted, during summer, by the fugitives from Charleston dust and fever, may be found, indeed, the bristly palmetto; but the whole island, with the exception of this western point, and a line of hard, white beach on the seacoast, is covered with a dense undergrowth of the sweet myrtle, so*

much prized by the horticulturists of England. The shrub here often attains the height of fifteen or twenty feet, and forms an almost impenetrable coppice, burthening the air with its fragrance.

The fort's stone walls, topped with a long row of cannons, rose up from one end of the island. The barracks were part of a roughly horseshoe-shaped set of structures. The officers stayed on one side with the enlisted men on the other. Poe would have slept on the second floor because the first floor was reserved for dining, cooking and storage.

The setting was not the biggest change for Poe. That spring, he became an artificer, the most technically demanding job in the army of his day, and assuming this position immediately doubled his pay. The nineteen-year-old was responsible for measuring, weighing and mixing explosives—an assignment so dangerous that any mistake could result in a loss of life or limbs. He would be tasked with filling a projectile with powder and then inserting a wick cut to the proper length to ensure that it detonated at just the right moment. Detonating too early could cause it to explode in midair or before leaving the cannon, killing or maiming at least the five men operating the weapon.

That Poe excelled in this task is obvious from the fact that he was not missing any arms or legs. His talent and intelligence were attracting the attention of his commanding officers; in particular, Lieutenant J. Howard took an interest in the young soldier, and Poe confided in him, revealing his true identity.

Not much else is known about Poe's life at Fort Moultrie. According to his commanding officers, he was invariably sober and hardworking. When he had the chance, he could have visited nearby Charleston. Poe also likely met the conchologist Dr. Edmund Ravenel on the island. Meeting the seashell expert could have led to Poe publishing a conchology textbook over a decade later.

According to legend, Poe also found time to fall in love with a local girl, the beautiful young Annabel Lee Ravenel. When her father forbade her to see the penniless soldier, the young lovers sneaked away to pledge their love for each other. When Poe was transferred to Fort Monroe, she fell into a depression that caused her to waste away and die. Blaming Poe for her fate, her father was determined to keep him from ever reuniting with her—even in death. Mr. Ravenel dug five different graves for her in the old Unitarian Church burying grounds, interred her in one and left them all unmarked. According to some old Charlestonians, she inspired Poe's poem "Annabel Lee."

To this day, Annabel Lee Ravenel's spirit is said to roam the burying grounds in search of her lost love. The legend has gotten so popular that the church has had to block access to the grounds after dark to keep out all the curious ghost hunters hoping to catch sight of her. This is despite the fact that there is no evidence that Annabel Lee Ravenel ever existed.

Another Sullivan's Island legend has it that Poe carved his name into a brick on Fort Moultrie's sallyport. A brick with Poe's initials *can* be found there, but it dates to well after his death.

However Poe occupied his free time, he likely devoted much of it to writing. The following year, he published another volume of poetry, so he probably wrote at least some of it while he was in South Carolina. ("Annabel Lee" was not among them.) That the aspiring poet was growing bored with military life and yearning to return to his old life is clear. He unburdened himself to Lieutenant Howard, who offered to let Poe out of his enlistment three years early if he could reconcile with John Allan. Since Poe had revealed his true age, he would need his guardian's consent for him to leave.

To this end, Howard sent a note to Allan in Richmond. The latter wrote back, "He had better remain as he is until the termination of his enlistment."

The poet replied to Allan on December 1, 1828, assuring him that Poe's rebellious youth was behind him. Poe continued,

> *You need not fear for my future prosperity—I am altered from what you knew me, & am no longer a boy tossing about on the world without aim or consistency—I feel that within me which will make me fulfil your highest wishes & only beg you to suspend your judgement until you hear of me again.*

Poe explained that he intended to continue his education at the United States Military Academy at West Point but could not do that until the termination of his enlistment.

> *I have been in the American army as long as suits my ends or my inclination, and it is now time that I should leave it—To this effect I made known my circumstances to Lieut Howard who promised me my discharge solely upon a re-conciliation with yourself—In vain I told him that your wishes for me (as your letters assured me) were, and had always been those of a father & that you were ready to forgive even the worst offences—He insisted upon my writing you & that if a re-conciliation*

could be effected he would grant me my wish. This was advised in the goodness of his heart & with a view of serving me in a double sense— He has always been kind to me, and, in many respects, reminds me forcibly of yourself.

Poe beseeched Allan for "a letter addressed to Lieut: J. Howard assuring him of your reconciliation with myself (which you have never yet refused) & desiring my discharge." This was all that stood between the poet and West Point.

VISITING FORT MOULTRIE

Fort Moultrie was also decommissioned, and it is now a National Historic Park. The fort has been restored to interpret different stages in its history from 1809 until 1947, but the barracks in which Poe lived have been demolished. The fort is located on one end of Sullivan's Island, which is now home to two thousand residents. If you go in the off-season, the island's beaches and trails might remind one of the natural beauty Poe encountered there nearly two centuries ago.

While the town has plenty of restaurants, the only choice for Poe pilgrims is Poe's Tavern. It is decorated with Poe-themed art, and some of the food has Poe-esque names like Edgar's Nachos, the Beef Raven and the Chicken Annabel Lee.

Nearby Gold Bug Island takes its name from Poe's tale "The Gold-Bug," which is set on Sullivan's Island. The area is home to the East Cooper Outboard Motor Club and can be rented for private events.

Getting to Sullivan's Island from downtown Charleston requires a car. It will take about half an hour to drive US-17 over the Ravenel Bridge and then follow SC-703 the rest of the way. Summer weekends draw a crowd, so plan accordingly.

Chapter 8

FORT MONROE, VIRGINIA

*J*ust over a year after Poe arrived at Sullivan's Island, his battery was transferred north to Fort Monroe in Virginia. It took about four days for them to reach the mouth of the Chesapeake Bay, where construction was underway on what would be the largest fort in the United States. The hexagonal bastioned fort would have ten-foot-thick stone walls surrounded by an eight-feet-deep moat. It would hold hundreds of cannons and thousands of soldiers, enough to protect the Chesapeake Bay; Washington, D.C.; and Baltimore from water invasion at a time when the burning of Washington by the British in the War of 1812 was still a recent memory.

By day, the air resounded with the rumble of construction and almost constant drilling. By night, the gentle waves lapped against the shore. Poe waited nearly three weeks for a response from Allan before writing again, hoping that his first letter had merely gotten lost in the mail. When there was still no reply, Poe asked his old Richmond friend John Mackenzie to visit Allan to make a personal appeal. After another month passed with no word from Allan, Poe sent him yet another letter, assuring the old man that there would be no difficulty in securing an appointment to West Point.

Convincing Allan that Poe had changed his ways since leaving the university was proving especially difficult with letters from his Charlottesville creditors still arriving at Moldavia from time to time. If Allan could not see that Poe had cleaned up his act, at least Poe's officers could. On January 1, 1829, he attained the rank of regimental sergeant major, something which

This photo taken around 1880 depicts the main gate at Fort Monroe. Although the fort was still under construction when Poe was stationed there, this gate had already been built, and Poe would have used it regularly.

usually took an average of seventeen years to accomplish. This bolstered Poe's confidence so much that he boasted to Allan that he could complete his West Point coursework in six months. While he continued to work as an artificer during the day, Poe spent his free time studying for West Point's entrance exams.

It was Poe's beloved foster mother who finally convinced Allan to respond to Poe. She was dying, and her last wish was to see her dear Edgar again. Tuberculosis claimed her on the last day of February. Her funeral was held four days later at Moldavia. From there, the horse-drawn hearse carried her coffin up Fifth Street to Shockoe Hill Cemetery, where she was buried within a stone's throw of Jane Stanard. Poe had just turned twenty, and the two women who had most supported and nurtured his talent during his early years were both gone.

He arrived in Richmond the evening after her burial, denying him the chance to look upon her face one last time. Back at Moldavia, he and Allan were civil. Allan said he forgave his wayward foster son for everything. It was a chance to reset their relationship and allow Poe to continue his education so that he might live a useful and productive life of public service.

Within days, Poe was back at Fort Monroe, securing letters of support from his officers, and Allan wrote to Charles Ellis's brother, U.S. Senator

Powhatan Ellis, to request another recommendation for Poe's West Point application. The letters from Poe's officers provide the best idea of Poe's personality and habits during his two years of military service. Lieutenant Howard wrote that Poe "at once performed the duties of company clerk and assistant in the Subsistent Department, both of which duties were promptly and faithfully done. His habits are good, and entirely free from drinking."

Lieutenant Henry W. Griswold found Poe "exemplary in his deportment, prompt & faithful in the discharge of his duties—and is highly worthy of confidence."

Lieutenant Colonel William T. Worth added that Poe's "deportment has been highly praise worthy & deserving of confidence. His education is of a very high order and he appears to be free from bad habits."

Before he could secure his discharge, Poe needed to find a replacement to fulfill the remainder of his enlistment. One of his fellow members of Battery H, Sergeant Samuel "Bully" Graves was about to end his enlistment and agreed to reenlist for the right price. Poe was so desperate to find a replacement that he offered Bully three times the usual price for a substitute. Although it was money he didn't have, Poe was certain that Allan would pay it. He was wrong.

Poe was discharged on April 15 and returned to Moldavia to continue collecting letters of recommendation. Many of Allan's friends composed glowing letters in praise of Poe's character and potential to distinguish himself at West Point. The only negative letter, and the only one that Poe could not exclude from his application, was John Allan's. In it, Allan begins by stating that Poe "left me in consequence of some Gambling at the university at Charlottesville." Allan continued, "Frankly Sir, do I declare that He is no relation to me whatever; that I have many [in] whom I have taken an active Interest to promote [theirs]; with no other feeling than that." After Poe had grown up under his roof, Allan was declaring that he cared no more for his ward than he would for any other child in need. In fact, Allan had paid for the education of at least one illegitimate son and would soon include two more in his will. Poe would be excluded from that document.

Poe did not stay long with the foster father who barely tolerated him. After leaving Moldavia, he traveled to Washington to deliver his accumulated letters of support to the Secretary of War John H. Eaton.

Rather than return to Richmond to await his appointment, Poe went to Baltimore. By this time, his longest poem, "Al Aaraaf," largely composed during his enlistment, was either complete or almost finished, and he started showing it to critics and publishers. After devoting all of his time and energy to securing admission to West Point, Poe's dream was still to achieve eminence in verse. As he wrote in May 1829 to the publisher Isaac Lea of Carey, Lea & Carey, "If ['Al Aaraaf'] is published, succeed or not, I am irrecoverably a poet."

In October, he wrote the editor John Neal, "I am young—not yet twenty—am a poet—if deep worship of all beauty can make me one—and wish to be so in the common meaning of the word. I would give the world to embody one half the ideas afloat in my imagination."

In the year that passed before Poe's admission to West Point, he searched for a publisher to release his second poetry collection, *Al Aaraaf, Tamerlane, and Other Poems*. Carey, Lea & Carey agreed to issue the book for $100, which was far more than Poe could afford. Hatch & Dunning offered a more reasonable deal to print about 500 copies, of which he would receive 250 to sell on his own. It was not a pretty book. The original boards were cheap, probably meant to be replaced by the buyer, who would hire a professional bookbinder to attach an attractive leather cover.

Reviews were mixed. In Baltimore's *Minerva and Emerald*, John Hill Hewitt opined, "'Al Aaraaf' is the title of the leading poem—of its object we have yet to be informed; for all our brain-cudgelling could not compel us to understand it line by line or the sum total."

In Boston's *American Monthly Magazine*, N.P. Willis described the enjoyment he experienced in watching Poe's poems burn in his fire. By contrast, in Boston's *Ladies' Magazine and Literary Gazette*, John Neal wrote that, while some of the poems "are exceedingly boyish, feeble, and altogether deficient in the common characteristics of poetry," others "remind us of no less a poet than [Percy] Shelley."

An anonymous critic writing for an unidentified Baltimore paper commented, "Throughout, there runs a rich vein of deep and powerful thought, clothed in language of almost inimitable beauty and harmony. His fancy is rich and of an elevated cast; his imagination powerfully creative."

Despite the publicity, the book did not make Poe either rich or famous, so, for the time being, his best option was West Point. While still waiting for his appointment, Poe received a letter from Bully Graves, looking for the money Poe owed him. Poe wrote back, "I have tried to get the money for you from Mr A[llan] a dozen times—but he always shuffles me off." Then Poe explained, "Mr A is not very often sober—which accounts for it."

VISITING FORT MONROE

Just like Forts Independence and Moultrie, Virginia's Fort Monroe has been decommissioned, but it is open to the public. Begin with a stop by the Fort Monroe Visitor and Education Center to pick up a map and a free ticket to the Casemate Museum. At the latter, you can go inside the largest stone fort in America. Watch your head because the ceilings are low in places. As you explore the exhibits, look out for a reference to Poe's time there and for the type of cannon he would have fired.

When you walk through the Main Gate, you will be entering the fort the same way Poe did, since it was the first portion to be constructed in 1820. Other structures from Poe's time include the Old Point Comfort Lighthouse (built in 1802) and Building #1, Old Quarters (built in 1819) and Building #17. If you plan ahead, you can register for the Fort Monroe Ghost Walk. If Poe's spirit fails to make an appearance (as he is said to have done on at least one occasion), you might catch sight of the ghost of a lady in white who is said to drift along the water's edge.

The best way to reach Fort Monroe is by car. From Norfolk and Virginia Beach to the east or from Richmond to the west, take I-64 to Exit 268. Turn left on South Mallory Street and then right on East Mellen Street.

Chapter 9

WEST POINT, NEW YORK

ot long after writing that letter, Poe departed Richmond for West Point, where he arrived in June 1830. Although only about fifty miles from New York City, the academy was as isolated as anywhere he had ever visited. From the city, it was only accessible by ship on the Hudson River. During the American Revolution, the academy's location had been used by the Continental army to protect northern New York from the British. Between the high bluffs rising over one thousand feet above the water and the sharp, narrow curves in the river, this was the perfect position from which to block the British ships from invading. It was because of the position's strategic importance to the war that the infamous traitor Benedict Arnold attempted to hand over the location to the British.

When the military academy opened there in 1802, the remote, nearly inaccessible location made it perfect for the sequestered learning environment the founders envisioned. This was to be a school in which there would be no distraction from one's studies nor tolerance for any violations of the rules. One such restriction that the poet gladly ignored forbade the possession of any poem unrelated to his studies.

In the center of campus was the academic building, which also contained a chapel on the first floor and a library on the second. On one side of this structure were two long three-story barracks for the cadets. Poe stayed in the South Barracks, a stone building about forty yards long with fifty rooms measuring about ten feet by thirteen feet each.

This 1834 engraving by John Archer shows the United States Military Academy at West Point as it appeared during Poe's time as a cadet. The widest building on the top center of the hill is the South Barracks, where Poe lived in Room 28.

The mess hall on the other side of the academic building ensured that the cadets consumed plenty of beef. It served baked, boiled, roasted, sliced, smoked or cold beef for breakfast, lunch and dinner with beef soup twice a week.

Poe earned a cadet's pay of sixteen dollars and two rations a month. It was over three times what he was paid when he first enlisted two years earlier, but it was still not enough for him and his roommates to keep their room supplied with brandy. They resorted to trading candles and blankets for alcohol.

In her extensive two-volume 1926 biography *Edgar Allan Poe: The Man*, Mary Phillips described Poe's uniform in detail:

> *A cadet's uniform was of blue cloth: single-breasted coat with standing collar, single herring-bone cuffs with one button on each, eight buttons in front, six on rear, and one on each side of the collar. Chapeau had a cockade, gilt eagle and loop. Half boots and shoes. Swords, cut and thrust, were worn in frog belt under the coat. Buttons were 3/8-inch, gilt, with eagle impressment.*

On the twenty-eighth of June, Poe wrote to Allan,

Upon arriving here I delivered my letters of [recommendation] *& was very politely received by Capn* [Ethan Allan] *Hitchcock & Mr Ross—The examination for admission is just over—a great many cadets of good family &c have been rejected as deficient....Of 130 Cadets appointed every year only 30 or 35 ever graduate—the rest being dismissed for bad conduct or deficiency the Regulations are rigid in the extreme.*

After passing the entrance exams, Poe went to camp, running drills in the hot sun until the end of August. Before returning to the academy, the cadets held a masquerade ball described in a letter from Cadet Jacob Bailey to his brother from that August 25, 1830:

The Cadets were all preparing when I arrived for a Grand Fancy Ball which there was last night....There was the usual number of...Beaux, Tailors, Sailors, Knights, Ladies, Devils, Bears, Baboons, Dandies, etc. etc. The character which was supported best of any that I saw was that of a Yankee from down East....There were many ladies present who were invited from Albany, Newburgh, and New York.

Life at the academy was extremely regimented, with the cadets rising at 5:00 a.m., running drills and parades for an hour and a half on five days a week and devoting the rest of the time to studying. Cadet David B. Harris described the schedule in a letter to his sister on April 11, 1830:

The cadets always go to bed at 1/2 past nine O'clock, and rise now at five; I have been in the habit during the winter of going to bed about two hours before tattoo [9:30 p.m.]*, and getting up at the same length of time before reveille, which I think is the best time for studying. We eat breakfast at seven O'clock and dinner at one throughout the year. The hours for study are from reveille until breakfast, from eight O'clock until dinner, from two O'clock until four, and from seven O'clock until tattoo. The 4th class recite in Mathematics from eight until 11 O'clock, and the 1st Section in French from two until three. We have to drill every evening except Saturday and Sunday evening from 10 minutes past four until about 1/2 past five O'clock. Parade takes place about 15 minutes past 6 O'clock, and we eat supper immediately after* *parade.... The battalion is inspected every Sunday when it is a fair day at 9 O'clock. The guard marches on immediately after inspection, and we go to church at 11 O'clock, and return at one; we have one hour of recreation from two until three O'clock on Sunday, and from three until parade it is study hours.*

During his first year, Poe studied French and mathematics. The latter included algebra, geometry, plane and spherical trigonometry and descriptive geometry. After distinguishing himself in French at the University of Virginia, he earned the third-highest score on his semi-annual French exam. He had the seventeenth-highest score, out of eighty-seven students, on his mathematics exam. After his disastrous year in Charlottesville, Poe's education was finally back on track.

He moved into Room 28 South Barracks with his roommates Thomas W. Gibson of Indiana and Timothy Pickering Jones of Tennessee. Both would soon be expelled for drunkenness, not such a remarkable feat when you consider that about one student a week was expelled for the same charge that fall. In all, 78 of the 102 members of Poe's class did not last until graduation. Not satisfied with an expulsion for mere drunkenness, Gibson decided to go out with a bang by setting fire to a campus building—after first disabling the nearby hydrants.

Years later, in the November 1867 issue of *Harper's New Monthly Magazine*, Gibson recalled, "Number 28 South Barracks, in the last months of the year of our Lord 1830, was pretty generally regarded as a hard room. Cadets who aspired to high standing on the Merit Roll were not much given to visiting it, at least in daytime." Although students were afraid to visit, the inspecting-officer Lieutenant Joseph Lorenzo Locke stopped by daily to hand out demerits for the infractions he inevitably found. A year older than Poe, Locke was the academy's assistant instructor of military tactics and was in charge of inspections, a position which made him feared and despised among the cadets. The reports he issued could—and did—result in expulsions. His visits must have been especially dreaded by Poe because the two knew each other from Fort Monroe, where the officer may have already taken a dislike to him.

To vent his frustrations, Poe penned some witty verses ridiculing the dreaded Locke. All that survives of the poem reads:

As for Locke, he is all in my eye,
May the d——l right soon for his soul call.

He never was known to lie—
In bed at a reveillé *roll-call.*

John Locke was a notable name;
Joe Locke is a greater: in short,
The former was well known to fame,
But the latter's well known "to report."

Poe quickly developed a reputation for humorous poems, ridiculing his officers, which he circulated among the cadets by means of his roommate Timothy Jones, who copied them with his left hand to disguise the handwriting and then hung them up around the academic building. These poems made Poe an object of fascination for some, like Jones, who told Woodberry that he considered Poe the "greatest fellow on earth" and spoke of his "literary genius."

When Poe regaled his classmates with stories of his life, he could not resist embellishing them more than a bit. As his fellow cadet David Emerson Hale wrote his mother, the editor Sarah Josepha Hale, whose magazine had previously called Poe's poems "boyish and feeble,"

> [Poe] *ran away from his adopted father in Virginia who was very rich, has been in S. America, England and has graduated at one of the Colleges there. He returned to America again and enlisted as a private soldier but feeling, perhaps a soldier's pride, he obtained a cadet's appointment and entered this Academy last June. He is thought a fellow of talent here but he is too mad a poet to like Mathematics.*

One of darkest rumors circulating about Poe—and one he might have been responsible for—was that he was the descendant of the very traitor who had attempted to turn over West Point to the British during the American Revolution. Poe seemed almost flattered when he wrote to John Allan that he had learned he was the grandson of Benedict Arnold.

Possibly the strangest story spreading around the academy about Poe was that, because he was a few years older that the other cadets (and looked much older than that), he was the father of a cadet who had secretly taken the place of his son who had died before the semester began. The rumors only grew with time until even his two roommates' accounts of him tend to contradict each other's. One, for example, stated that Poe was rarely sober while the other claimed never to have seen Poe intoxicated.

The stories that have become legendary relate to Poe's penchant for malicious pranks. In the previously mentioned *Harper's* article, Thomas Gibson recounted the events of one cold November night in Room 28. The roommates had run out of brandy and needed to sneak off campus to trade some of their candles for another bottle. They drew straws to see who would have to make the trip, and Gibson lost. He would have to grope through the pitch-black woods and down the hill to an off-campus establishment down by the banks of the Hudson where a tavern owner named Benny Haven could be relied on to supply cadets with alcohol. When Gibson reached Benny Haven's place, he picked up a bottle of brandy and a goose, the head of which Old Benny chopped off for him.

Fortifying himself with a drink or two, Gibson staggered home through the darkness with the goose over his shoulder, dripping blood down his shirt. To help him avoid the officer or townsperson identified in the account as Old K——, Poe met Gibson on the road and guided him back to the South Barracks, where their friends had gathered. The blood saturating Gibson's shirt gave Poe an idea. Gibson would arrive, stumbling as if in a daze. Poe would ask him what the matter was, and Gibson would "confess" to having encountered Old K—— on the road, gotten into an altercation with him and chopped off his head. When Poe feigned disbelief, Gibson would reply, "I didn't suppose you would believe me, so I cut off his head and brought it into barracks. Here it is!" At this, Gibson would pull out a bloody knife and the goose while blowing out the room's only candle.

The stunt worked so well that one of their guests leaped out a window and fled. It took several minutes for another guest to recover from the fright. The next night, the roommates cut up and cooked the goose, claiming they were eating Old K—— in effigy.

More unverifiable tales of Poe's other hijinks have turned up over the years. The most popular of these exist in a few different forms, and the essential elements are that Poe was told not to forget to wear his sword to parade the next day. When the time came, he arrived wearing nothing but his sword. Regardless of the many who truly want to believe this story, it can be traced back only as far as the 1920s. Like most of the stories associated with Poe's time at West Point, it is surely a myth.

We can, however, construct a picture of his living conditions and how they might have affected him. Just like Charlottesville, when he lived on Rowdy Row, Poe found himself residing in the "party dorm." Although Poe began the semester distinguishing himself in French and mathematics, Jones told Poe's biographer George Edward Woodberry that something happened a few weeks later that caused him "to lose interest in his studies and to be disheartened and discouraged."

The source of Poe's discouragement was something that happened miles away in New York. Just a month into Poe's first semester, John Allan remarried. After Frances Allan's sister declined his proposal, Allan courted a woman twenty-one years his junior, Louisa Gabriella Patterson, whom he married on October 5 in New York. Poe wrote to Allan on November 6, expressing disappointment that his foster father had not bothered to visit him while in area, a sign that Allan no longer wanted anything to do with the child he had only taken in for Frances's sake. Now Allan would have a new family and legitimate heirs. In an effort to prove he had changed his ways, Poe reassured the older man, "I have a very excellent standing in my class," but it was too late. Poe's instincts were correct. There was to be no mention of him in Allan's will.

What Poe did not yet know is that Allan was furious with Poe for calling him a drunkard in that last letter to Bully Graves. At some point, Graves showed Allan Poe's letter, which was later found among Allan's papers. Allan fired off an angry letter in response, informing his wayward foster son to never contact him again.

By this time, Poe was losing patience with the constant drills, parades, guard duty and rules. During his enlistment, he had avoided most of these responsibilities, but they were now inescapable. While he had proven himself more than capable of excelling in his classes, he wanted to rebel against the military disciple and duties. Poe also wanted to resume his writing career. His poem "Sonnet—To Science" had appeared in both the *Saturday Evening Post* and the *Casket* while Poe was at West Point, his satirical poems had been a hit with his classmates and he was hard at work on a new book of poetry. Over one hundred of the cadets agreed to help pay for its publication.

Deciding it was time to leave, Poe requested Allan's permission to resign. As Poe's legal guardian, Allan needed to consent to the plan. On January 3, 1831—the first day of midterm exams—Poe wrote Allan a long letter listing his grievances, blaming Allan for not providing enough money to pay for tuition at the University of Virginia and admitting to writing the letter to Bully Graves:

> As regards Sergt. Graves—I did *write him that letter. As to the truth of its contents, I leave it to God, and your own conscience.—The time in which I wrote it was within a half hour after you had embittered every*

feeling of my heart against you by your abuse of my family, *and myself, under your own roof—and at a time when you knew that my heart was almost breaking.*

Poe concludes by making a final appeal for permission to resign, throwing in a last guilt trip and threatening to get himself thrown out of the academy if he does not hear back from Allan within ten days. Poe did not wait that long to stop attending classes or drills. Joe Locke dutifully reported all his infractions until Poe was court-martialed.

Rather than respond to Poe, Allan wrote on the letter's margin, "I do not think the Boy has one good quality. He may do or act as he pleases, tho' I wd have saved him but on his own terms & conditions since I cannot believe a word he writes. His letter is the most barefaced one sided statement."

By the end of the month, Poe appeared before the court-martial accused of thirty-two counts of "gross neglect of duty" and two counts of "disobeyance of orders." The court found him guilty of all charges and expelled him from the academy, effective on March 6, 1831. He headed for New York with little more than the clothes on his back and lacking a cloak to keep him warm. He caught a cold that left him bedridden for days. Just when all seemed lost, he received a check from West Point. Out of the 232 cadets, 139 had contributed $1.25 each from their pay to help Poe publish his next volume of poetry.

That spring, the publisher Elam Bliss issued his book *Poems*, which he dedicated to "The U.S. Corps of Cadets." It is significant that over half of his fellow cadets and at least one of his officers believed in Poe's talents enough to help fund his dream. When the subscribers' copies arrived at West Point, the cadets snatched up their books to find out how he had lampooned their officers. For once, his readers actually *wanted* him to write something funny. They finally appreciated his sense of humor. Naturally, he sent them a book full of melancholy poems about dead lovers and decaying corpses instead. The cadets threw most of their copies into the Hudson River, and Poe became the butt of their jokes for years to come.

Thomas Gibson later wrote,

The book was received with a general expression of disgust. It was a puny volume, of about fifty pages, bound in boards and badly printed on coarse paper, and worse than all, it contained not one of the squibs and satires upon which his reputation at the Academy had been built up.

Cadet Ben Hardin (who was also destined to be expelled) summed up the general sentiment when he wrote on the flyleaf of his copy, "This book is a damn cheat. All that fills 124 pages could have been compiled in 36."

Of course, hindsight tells us that the poems in this volume were his best to date. Some of them would evolve, through a few revisions, to become his classics "Lenore," "Israfel," "To Helen" and "The Valley of Unrest." It was with Poe's third book that he came into his own, that he published the poems we recognize as his mature work—and he had only just turned twenty-one. The volume would not make him rich or famous, so, for now, he would need to find employment. To that end, he moved to live with his relatives in Baltimore. That is the subject of our next chapter.

Shortly after leaving West Point, Poe wrote the superintendent of the U.S. Military Academy, Colonel Sylvanus Thayer, to reveal his latest plan—Poe wanted to join the Polish fight for independence from Russia. Poe asked if Thayer might contact the Marquis de Lafayette on his behalf. There is no record of how long Thayer laughed after reading it.

Thus ended Poe's military career. While he boasted of his West Point training and wore his old West Point greatcoat for the rest of his life (it appears in two daguerreotypes of him), he pretended the two years of his enlistment never happened. Instead, he told everyone that he had gone to Europe after leaving the University of Virginia. This is the story that appears in articles about him published during his lifetime. It was not until almost four decades after Poe's death that his biographer George Edward Woodberry found the records proving where he really was between 1827 and 1829. But it should have been obvious after Poe used Sullivan's Island as the setting for his mystery "The Gold-Bug." Aside from a few alterations, his descriptions of the island were so accurate that a reader might guess he had actually lived there. Poe also used it as a setting in both "The Balloon Hoax" and "The Oblong Box."

VISITING WEST POINT

West Point is an active-duty military post, so there are a lot of rules concerning visits by civilians. Be sure to check their website to see what you will need to do to visit. You might consider taking a West Point bus tour. More information is available at westpointtours.com. Even with the tour, you will probably need a background check, so visit their website for more information.

If you do get to see the campus, you will not find Poe's dorm room because the South Barracks in which he stayed were demolished in the 1850s. To make matters worse, a fire consumed the original academic building in 1838, so the structures in which Poe spent most of his time at West Point have been lost. At least there is a plaque marking the site of Benny Haven's tavern at the corner of Main Street and Cozzens Avenue in nearby Highland Falls.

Chapter 10

POE HOUSE AND MUSEUM, BALTIMORE

*T*oday it is one of Baltimore's most important attractions. Sure, it might not see as many Poe pilgrims as Poe's grave does, but his home on Amity Street is the place to go to meet the poet, to walk in his footsteps and—just maybe—feel his presence. Stories abound of the spirits that roam its hallowed halls, and at least one visitor ran out the front door screaming that she would never return. None other than horror film legend Vincent Price said, "This place gives me the creeps!" The only thing more terrifying than this house is just how close it came to being demolished.

Situated on the outskirts of Baltimore, the cramped rowhouse was only half of a double house, both of which were about as deep as Poe could have leaped with a running start. On climbing the front steps, one enters a small, dark parlor that leads to another, even smaller, kitchen. A steep, narrow staircase leads upstairs to two bedrooms, one of which Poe probably shared with his cousin. Another staircase, this one so steep that you might be tempted to climb it on all fours to keep from tripping, takes you to the tiniest bedroom, a space so small that a tall child standing up in the center would crack his skull on the sloping ceiling with a single step to the right or the left. Some Poe fans like to believe this claustrophobia-inducing garret was Poe's bedroom, but it was more likely that of his nine-year-old cousin Virginia. The house is a little bigger today—but not much.

The place was one of only three newly built homes on its block when Poe's invalid grandmother Elizabeth Poe (not to be confused with Poe's mother, Elizabeth Poe, or his aunt Elizabeth Poe) rented it. She was the widow of a local Revolutionary War hero, General David Poe, who, while never actually a general, had been an honorary quartermaster general of Baltimore and a friend of the Marquis de Lafayette. As a quartermaster, David Poe supplied the Continental troops with food, clothing, weapons and transportation. When the soldiers ran low on pants, Elizabeth Poe stepped forward to organize the sewing of five hundred pairs. When the supplies ran low, David started replenishing them with his own money. Taking out loan after loan, he ended up spending $40,000 (estimated at nearly $1 million 2024 dollars). If he expected the U.S. government

Pictured here is the house in which Poe lived in Baltimore when he published his first horror story, "Berenice," in 1835. The photograph was taken after the left half of the house was removed by developers in 1941. Now the building is operated as the Poe House and Museum of Baltimore.

to repay him after it won the war, he was sorely disappointed. Only after his death, and following many failed petitions, was his widow able to receive some form of compensation.

This repayment amounted to an annual pension of a couple hundred dollars, which was just enough to ensure that all of her poorest relatives took up residence under her roof. Among these was Edgar Poe's alcoholic, tubercular brother, William Henry Leonard Poe, who died a year before she moved to the new house. Then there was her daughter (and Edgar's aunt) the widow Maria Poe Clemm, as well as the latter's son Henry and daughter Virginia. Joining them was the recently expelled West Point cadet Edgar Poe.

By the time he moved to Baltimore, reviews of his latest volume of poems were beginning to circulate—and they

This daguerreotype taken in 1849 depicts Edgar Allan Poe's beloved aunt and mother-in-law, Maria Poe Clemm, whom he called Muddy and to whom he addressed the poem "To My Mother." While she was dedicated to her son-in-law, she also stole a volume he had borrowed and sold it behind his back.

weren't kind. While a few offered some slight encouragement for the young author, others savaged his weird verse. It would be fourteen years before he published another volume of his poems.

In the meantime, the depressed author attempted to support himself with whatever jobs he could find. Rumor has it that he might have worked as a bricklayer, an appropriate inspiration for his tales of sealing people behind walls in "The Black Cat" and "The Cask of Amontillado." He is also reputed to have worked in a kiln and helped out at one of the local newspaper offices. He even tried—and failed—to get a teaching job.

Ultimately, he remained determined to find fame with his pen. If poetry was not going to get him there, then he would turn to fiction. A few months before he moved to the Amity Street house, he had entered a short story contest sponsored by a Philadelphia newspaper called the *Saturday Courier*. Although he had not yet published any fiction, he was convinced he could write a good enough tale to bring home the prize. He had no other choice. With his debts growing and his prospects fading with each increasingly pathetic appeal for aid from John Allan, Poe needed the fifty-dollar prize more than ever. In a desperate move to increase his odds, Poe submitted not one but five of his best tales.

He lost the contest. But the worst part is that the paper published all of his submissions anyway—without paying him. Since the paper was in another city, he might not have even known he had gotten his first short story published.

Unable to secure employment, Poe sent one more groveling letter to Allan:

> *It has now been more than two years since you have assisted me, and more than three since you have spoken to me.... Without friends, without any means, consequently of obtaining employment, I am perishing— absolutely perishing for want of aid. And yet I am not idle—nor addicted to any vice—nor have I committed any offence against society which would render me deserving of so hard a fate. For God's sake pity me, and save me from destruction.*

Back in Richmond, Allan filed away the letter but did not reply. Instead, he noted on one of Poe's other letters,

> *Apl 12, 1833 it is now upwards of 2 years since I received the above precious relict of the Blackest Heart & deepest ingratitude alike destitute of honour & principle every day of his life has only served to confirm his debased nature—Suffice it to say my only regret is in Pity for his failings—his Talents are of an order that can never prove a comfort to their possessor.*

Poe was in search of another option, and he needed to find it soon. He managed to sell a few of his poems to a local newspaper, but he was making far less than Maria earned for sewing dresses. He then sent one of his tales to Boston's *New-England Magazine*, which rejected it.

In the second-floor bedroom he shared with his cousin Henry, Poe jotted down draft after draft of new tales and poems in his microscopic script. He composed the final drafts of his stories in a print handwriting so neat it almost looks typed. His next project was a proposed collection of short fiction to be called *Eleven Tales of the Arabesque*. Once again, this project failed to pan out.

In these lean times, Poe's grandmother was fading quickly. Maria took up carrying an empty pot to relatives' homes to beg them to fill it with any scraps she could transform into a stew. Fourteen-year-old Henry was probably working as a stonecutter. But Edgar was still trying to find his place in the world.

Unable to secure a teaching job, Poe began tutoring Virginia. The two grew so close that he started calling her Sissy, as if she were the kid sister he never had, and she called him Buddy. He also took to calling Maria Clemm Muddy, as if she were also his mother. Virginia acted as his messenger, often turning up on the doorsteps of Baltimore ladies to deliver his love poems.

Since arriving in Baltimore, Poe had fallen in love with his cousin Eliza Rebecca Herring before her father forbade the match. He turned his attention to Kate Bleakley, the daughter of a hotel manager, but was spurned again. About the time he moved to the Amity Street house, he set his sights on the auburn-haired Mary Starr. As she told it half a century later, she and Poe blew kisses and waved handkerchiefs at each other from their bedroom windows before they finally met in person. Then he sent Sissy to her house to request a lock of her hair, and Mary complied.

When the time came to meet, Poe was passing Mary's parents' house and spotted her sitting on her porch. The seventeen-year-old Mary turned away, too shy to risk making eye contact with him, so he made himself impossible to ignore by leaping over the railing to join her on the porch. He rhapsodized over her auburn locks. According to Mary, in an interview she gave to Augustus Van Cleef for the March 1889 issue of *Harper's New Monthly Magazine*, "He told me I had the most beautiful head of hair he ever saw, the hair that poets always raved about."

In the same article, she recounted that Poe "was handsome, but intellectually so, not a pretty man. He had the way and the power to draw any one to him. He was very fascinating, and any young girl would have fallen in love with him." She said that Poe pleaded with her to marry him, and she might have agreed had he not shown up drunk one night on her doorstep.

Scholars have debated how much of Mary's self-serving version of events bears any resemblance to the truth. Although the poems he dedicated to Eliza Herring survive, the ones he supposedly addressed to Mary Starr are lost.

Back at the Amity Street house, Poe read that a local paper, the *Saturday Visiter*, would be hosting a writing contest. The author of the best tale would win fifty dollars, and the best poem would earn twenty-five. Confident he could win both divisions, Poe submitted his poem "The Coliseum" along with a selection of his best short stories. Once again, Poe was risking losing his stories. If the *Visiter* printed them without paying him, they would be all but impossible to sell. Most other papers would not pay for a previously published story when, due to the lax copyright laws of the day, they could just print those works for free. Given the difficulty he had met in selling his works so far, the contest was worth the risk.

The contest runners were confronted with mountains of paper covered with oftentimes illegible poems and short stories submitted by aspiring authors, each as desperate as Poe was to catch his or her big break. The table strained under the weight of these pages as the illustrious judges gathered around it. As they were discussing how to embark on this process of reading the entries, narrowing down the finalists and selecting the winners, one of the judges spotted an especially neat little sheath of paper adorned by tiny and immaculate handwriting as legible as if it were printed. One of Poe's enemies, Rufus Griswold, later claimed that the judges selected Poe's story only because the handwriting was so neat that they did not bother to read the other entries. While Poe's handwriting might have caught their attention, it surely did not prevent them from reading any of the other entries.

After reading Poe's contributions, the judges' decision to make was which of his five entries deserved the prize for best short story. They ultimately selected "MS Found in a Bottle," an adventure yarn about a man who finds himself trapped aboard a ghost ship.

For the poetry contest, they agreed that Poe deserved the prize but were hesitant to award it to him since he had already won the short story division. The fiction prize was worth twice as the poetry award, so they decided to give him the higher amount. Meanwhile, they gave the poetry prize to "The Song of the Winds" by Henry Wilton. The latter was actually a pseudonym for John Hill Hewitt, who was on the *Visiter*'s staff. Incensed at the possibility that Hewitt had cheated, Poe confronted him on the street and told him as much. Fists started flying, and a bloody, bruised Poe stumbled back home to Amity Street.

The prize was a lifeline for Poe. A week at his writing desk had brought him what it would have taken him months to earn at the brick kiln. While he was by no means wealthy, he could pay off his debts and help support Muddy and her family. More importantly, the prize served as an introduction to one of the contest's judges, John Pendleton Kennedy, the popular novelist who was in a position to connect Poe with editors and publishers. Kennedy invited Poe to his home, provided him a horse to ride and loaned him money.

It wasn't long before Poe first saw one of his tales in a national magazine. Unfortunately, this particular story did not make much of an impression. It was "The Visionary," the romance that the *Visiter* judges had previously rejected. In the tale, a dark, Byronic hero (based as much on Lord Byron as on how Poe wanted himself to be seen) loves the most beautiful woman in Venice, but she is married to an older, richer man for whom she has no affection. Unable to fulfil their desires, they commit suicide. It is easy to see reflections of Poe's unrequited love for Elmira, herself married to an older, richer man, in this narrative.

If Elmira was on his mind when he wrote the story, she was rapidly fading from his memory. In the little house on Amity Street, Eddie's interest in Sissy was evolving, but we know frustratingly little about their relationship at this time. No letters between Edgar and Virginia from this period exist, but one written by Poe to Maria and Virginia from Richmond in 1835 reveals how close their bond had become. He wrote to Maria, "I love, you know I love Virginia passionately devotedly. I cannot express in words the fervent devotion I feel towards my dear little cousin—my own darling."

Although this portrait is said to depict Edgar Allan Poe's wife and cousin Virginia Clemm, the identification is rejected by most Poe scholars. When it was offered to the Poe Museum in the 1930s, the collections committee declined it because it could not be authenticated. It is now owned by a private collector.

In a postscript, Poe addresses Virginia as "My love, my own sweetest Sissy, my darling little wifey." Whatever the nature of their relationship, her mother condoned and even encouraged it. She probably discussed it with her many relatives in the area because her stepdaughter Josephine Poe eventually determined to take Virginia into her own home rather than let her marry Edgar. Josephine considered Virginia too young to get married. Twelve-year-olds were allowed to marry with their father's consent, but this law was a throwback to the days when lifespans were considerably shorter. By Poe's time, the average woman in the United States did not marry until she was twenty.

There was no evidence that Poe married Virginia while they were living in Baltimore. Despite a rumor to the contrary that identified both the location of the ceremony and the supposed minister performing it, there is no record connecting either the church or the officiant to the event. It is more likely that Edgar *considered* himself engaged to Virginia. Just as he had with Elmira Royster nearly a decade earlier, Poe's courtship involved long walks in the fresh country air.

A friend, Wilmer Lambert, later described joining Edgar and Virginia on one of these strolls around the city. When the trio approached a stranger's funeral, Virginia was so overcome with grief that she sobbed more passionately than any of the deceased's friends or family. Edgar, in turn, was affected by Virginia's tears and started crying along with her over the freshly dug grave.

Cemeteries in Baltimore were encountering some of the same problems as those in Charlottesville and Richmond. Their residents did not always stay put. During Poe's time in the Charm City, another grave-robbing scandal hit the papers. This time, dentists were stealing corpses' teeth to make dentures. Poe and his literary friends were discussing the case when one of them bet Poe that even he could not write a story about something so unbelievable, so grotesque, so disturbing. Never one to turn down a good bet, Poe set out to write a tale titled "The Teeth." In it, a man becomes so obsessed with his wife's smile that, after she grows ill and is buried in the family cemetery, he digs up her body and extracts her teeth. Only after he awakens covered in mud and gore does he realize that she had been accidentally buried alive and, one imagines, was not happy about having her teeth removed. The piece ends with the sight of her thirty-two blood-speckled teeth spilling across the floor.

Poe added "The Teeth" to the table of contents of his still unpublished short story collection, which he now called *Tales of the Folio Club*. The collection would be framed by an account of members of a literary society telling each other stories. Between each tale, the members would make humorous comments about the preceding work. He compiled all the tales, written in his precise print handwriting, into a small notebook.

After three failed volumes of poetry, Poe still considered publishing books to be the best way to make his reputation, but ever since getting his first tales published in the *Saturday Courier*, it was growing increasingly apparent that his work was better suited for magazines. The periodicals were willing to pay cash for his stories while book publishers often demanded their authors contribute to the cost of printing. His shift in focus from books to magazines was complete when one of the *Saturday Visiter* contest judges, John Pendleton Kennedy, informed him of an opportunity to help edit the *Southern Literary Messenger*, a new magazine founded in Richmond.

Poe jumped at the chance to earn a steady paycheck from his writing. For his first contribution, he sent the publisher Thomas Willis White his tooth story, now titled "Berenice." Poe considered it the best example of his writing, and it was definitely the best previously unpublished work he had available.

Maybe White was so desperate to fill the pages of his magazine that he inserted the story without reading it. After all, publication was running so far behind schedule that the February 1835 issue was not released until March 15, and the March issue, the one to which Poe submitted "Berenice," would not reach subscribers until April 17. If he had read the tale, White might have removed some of the most offensive passages (ones which Poe himself later cut before anthologizing it) or declined to run the work altogether. It offended enough readers that, within two weeks of publication, Poe wrote White an apology and admitted that "the subject is by far too horrible" but explained that stories just such as this would make the *Southern Literary Messenger* a success.

History has since proved Poe right. Not only did his tales boost the magazine's circulation, but they also brought Poe national recognition. The magazine operated for three more decades, but the only pieces published in its pages that are still widely read today are Poe's.

With his possible engagement to Virginia on his mind, he had made an account of teeth-robbing into a tale of an unhappy marriage between an obsessive and self-centered husband and his neglected wife. His follow-up for the *Messenger*'s April issue was about another miserable marriage. In "Morella," the narrator's wife despises him so much that she threatens to return from the dead to torment him.

Poe also submitted seventeen literary notices to the same issue. He was now a regular contributor of tales, poems and book reviews. But every issue was still coming out about a month behind schedule. White needed immediate help editing the *Messenger* to get back on deadline and invited Poe to join him in Richmond.

This was the opportunity to earn a living from his pen that Poe had been waiting for, but his timing could not have been worse. His grandmother and sole source of support for the entire household, Elizabeth Cairnes Poe, died in July of that year. Although only about 8 percent of the $40,000 her husband had spent supplying the Continental army had been repaid through her annual pension, the government refused to transfer the pension to her heirs. Maria and Virginia were destitute. Their last hope was for Edgar to establish himself at the *Messenger* and to set up a home in Richmond for them.

Elizabeth's funeral took place in the tiny home on Amity Street, probably in the room that now houses the museum's gift shop. About a week later, Poe set off for the Virginia capital, well aware that the only family he had left desperately needed him to succeed.

The pressure was almost too much to bear. Poe started drinking heavily. When he received a letter the following month from Maria Clemm saying that Josephine Clemm and her husband, Neilson, a wealthy lawyer, had offered to take Virginia and Maria into their home, Poe poured out his heart to her in a tear-drenched letter pleading with them to join him in Richmond instead. He fled to Baltimore, causing White to fire him.

Ultimately, Poe's aunt and cousin gave up a comfortable life with Josephine and Nielson to follow Edgar through uncharted territory—the treacherous path to becoming the first major American author to support himself entirely from his writing. The odds were not in Poe's favor. Most authors of his day were attorneys, professors, diplomats or customshouse officials who could devote their free time to writing. But Poe saw the explosion of American magazines as his ticket to fame and fortune. It would all begin with the *Southern Literary Messenger*, if Maria and Virginia had only the courage to follow him. While the rest of his life would be devoted to their care, they were sacrificing everything to support him. Along the way, it would be their contributions, including Maria's management of Poe's business affairs and the household budget, that would make Poe's literary career possible. But first he needed to convince White to give him a second chance.

THE POE HOUSE AFTER POE

After Edgar, Maria and Virginia moved out of the Amity Street house, it went through a succession of owners, and the significance of the place was forgotten. This is where Poe was living when he became a short story writer. It was here that he turned from writing books of poetry to contributing fiction for magazines. Most importantly, it was here that he forever bound himself to Maria and Virginia Clemm.

Fourteen years later, Poe died while passing through Baltimore on his way from Richmond to Philadelphia. Neilson Poe and Edgar's cousin Elizabeth Herring, now Elizabeth Herring Smith, were among the handful of friends and relatives to attend his funeral on that cold, drizzly October after when they laid him to rest near General Poe's grave.

That unmarked grave, neglected and overgrown with weeds, soon attracted such a flood of Poe pilgrims that the sexton who had buried the poet found himself playing the part of a tour guide for all the literary lovers and aspiring authors in search of the raven's resting place. To help him remember where it was, he placed a stone over the spot. This served as Poe's only monument for the first twenty-six years after his death.

For over half a century, Poe pilgrims were far more interested in visiting what was left of the poet's bones than they were in seeing the house in which he had once lived and worked. Poe specialists knew the house's general location, but it was far from the kind of landmark that Washington's and Jefferson's homes had become.

It was the City of Baltimore that ultimately forced Poe's admirers to step forward to save the site. In 1941, the Poe house was scheduled for demolition to make way for a new housing development. When the Poe Society beseeched the city to spare the site, it agreed on the conditions that the organization must conclusively identify Poe's house and that the city would spare only half of the double house. This meant that the Poe society had to scramble to determine which half of the house was which before the city demolished both. Journalist and Poe Society member May Garrettson Evans searched old maps and property records, factoring in that the addresses on the houses had changed over time. Just in time, she determined which side of the double house was occupied by the Poes and Clemms, and the city tore down the other half.

With the Poe house definitively identified and out of danger, it survived for decades as a literary landmark. In fact, it was more than a landmark. It was a place of pride for the neighborhood and the city to celebrate its most famous resident. (My apologies to all the other writers, artists, filmmakers, politicians and athletes who have called the Charm City their home, but which of you has Baltimore's football team named after one of their poems?) Over time, the kids who grew up reading Poe's horror stories in school came to associate that ancient structure with all things dark and mysterious. The September 18, 1999 issue of the *Baltimore Sun* reported that neighborhood children feared the place and thought that Poe's ghost jumped from rooftop to rooftop at night, terrorizing kids.

In *Ghosts of Virginia, Volume 3*, L.B. Taylor records that on November 10, 1979, the psychic John Krysko visited the house and revealed that Poe's ghost still roams the house in search of a lost manuscript. Krysko said that a security guard told him of seeing a flickering light, like a candle, moving slowly and deliberately about the house when nobody (living) should have been there. The same moving light was witnessed by a neighbor during a 1968 power outage.

One witness peered into the house through a window and thought he saw a shadowy form sitting at a writing desk. Others claim to have seen a female spirit. Still another, an actor who was dressing in an upstairs bedroom for a performance in the house during Jeff Jerome's time as the curator, saw a window frame rise up and out of its groove and fly across the room. The actor skipped the performance and never returned. Ever since, people have occasionally admitted to feeling watched while in that room.

With all the people who have lived and died in that house since Poe's time, is there any chance that Poe's is among the spirits in residence? In 2012, Jerome decided to find out by inviting a group of paranormal investigators to search the house. They spent a night sitting in dark rooms, asking questions in hopes that a response would show up on their audio or video recordings, but, if he was there, Poe was not very talkative.

VISITING THE POE HOUSE

The Poe House and Museum is administered by Poe Baltimore and is open to the public, but you will need to make a reservation because the site is small. Be sure to check their website for hours and to make a reservation. Also, make sure you are on the Poe Baltimore website (poeinbaltimore.org) because some people accidentally make reservations at the Poe Museum in Richmond and are very confused when they arrive at the Baltimore

Poe House with tickets for the wrong site. It happens more often than you might think.

Once you have made your reservation, you can reach the Poe House at 203 North Amity Street by car or by bus. If you are driving from the north from Washington, D.C., or Richmond, take I-95 North to Exit 53 for I-395 North. Follow signs to Martin Luther King Jr. Boulevard, which you will take to West Fayette Street. Turn left on Fayette and right on North Schroeder Street, right on West Saratoga Street and right on North Amity Street. The Poe House will be at the end of the block on the left. There is no parking lot, but you can find parking spots on the street. Be sure to lock your vehicle and keep any valuables out of sight, but you should probably do that whenever you park.

If you are coming from the west, take I-70 East to I-695 South to I-95 North to Exit 53 and follow the directions above. If you are traveling from the east, you can take I-95 South to Exit 53. If you are coming from the north, you can take I-83 (Jones Falls Expressway) south to the St. Paul Street exit. Then take St. Paul Street to Chase Street and turn right. That becomes Martin Luther King Jr. Boulevard, which you will follow south to West Fayette Street and turn right. The rest is the same as above.

If you are already in Baltimore, you can get to the Poe House from the Inner Harbor on the free Charm City Circulator Orange Line. Stop 210 is the closest one to the Poe House. You can also walk from Inner Harbor, but wear comfortable shoes because it will be one and a half miles. Take Pratt Street west, turn right onto Charles Street, left at Fayette Street and right onto North Amity Street. The Poe house will be north of Lexington Street, on the right.

When you reach the house with your ticket, you will have to wait outside for the tour to begin. They will not let you enter early because they allow only sixteen guests at a time. You will find out why once you are inside.

Entering the house will be worth the wait. Among the Poeana to see are Poe's lap desk and telescope, but the main thing to experience is the house itself. The cramped quarters and narrow stairs will transport you back into those early, desperate days when Poe struggled to launch a writing career. You can envision him sitting next to the window, scribbling down "Berenice," "MS Found in a Bottle," or "Morella" with a quill pen on paper he could scarcely afford.

Once you have experienced the Poe House, your Baltimore Poe pilgrimage will not be complete without seeing Poe's grave. Fortunately, it is only a short walk or drive away. Walk south on Fayette Street, and you will be there in fifteen minutes where it intersects Green Street. The Enoch Pratt Free Library also has a considerable Poe collection that includes such pieces as a Valentine's poem written by Virginia to Edgar, a piece of Poe's coffin and some of Poe's letters. There is usually a selection of Poe books in the Poe Room on the second floor of the Main Branch at 400 Cathedral Street. Once again, check their website to make sure the Poe Room will be open when you are in town because it is sometimes booked for private meetings. Better still, make an appointment to view some of the Poe items that are not normally on display.

Chapter 11

MRS. YARRINGTON'S
BOARDING HOUSE,
RICHMOND

Thomas White was desperate. Finding a replacement for his young editor would not be easy, so he decided to give Poe one more chance. Poe could return to the *Messenger* if he quit drinking and his "bottle companions." Poe got back to work writing editorials and book reviews in addition to printing some of his own stories and poems in the magazine. His salary was about forty-three dollars per month, enough for him to live comfortably without luxury.

This allowed Poe to rent a room in a three-story brick boardinghouse with a wide granite staircase rising above the English basement to the front door. From their window in the second-floor room over the front door, they had an unobstructed view of the majestic columned portico of Jefferson's Capitol looming over them from the summit of Capitol Hill. To the right of the capitol, closer to the bottom of the square, they could see the Virginia Museum directly across the street from them. Poe already well knew this view from the many times he had visited that house during his childhood. Often, when angry with John Allan, Poe had climbed up an adjacent tree and into his best friend Ebenezer Burling's window to spend the night. In those days, Burling's mother was operating her own boardinghouse there.

Barely eight years earlier, Poe and Burling had stowed away on a coal ship together with dreams of seeing the world. Burling's courage faltered at Norfolk and he returned to Richmond, leaving Poe to seek his fortune alone. They would never see each other again. When Poe was living in Baltimore, Burling fell victim to the global cholera pandemic that terrorized much of Asia, Africa, Europe and the Americas in the 1830s. In a matter of days, victims suffered from abdominal pain, vomiting and such intense diarrhea that they became dehydrated, their skin turning bluish gray and their faces sunken and skeletal.

In Baltimore, Poe had watched wagons carrying corpses to mass graves, a grim sight familiar in major cities throughout the fledgling nation. He could hear the creak of wooden wagon wheels, the sobs of the grieving and the voices of temperance advocates and ministers who preached that this plague was God's punishment for the city's sinister ways. Doctors and moralists urged citizens to abandon immoral behavior and alcohol in favor of clean living and fresh water. Regrettably, cholera spread through the water. In those days, many took their water for drinking and cleaning

Painted about 1900, this miniature watercolor on ivory is thought to represent Poe at the age of twenty-six, when he joined the staff of the *Southern Literary Messenger* as editor and literary critic.

from the same streams, ditches or wells where they cleaned the soiled linens of the infected.

Fortunately, doctors came to the rescue by administering medicines made from mercury, ground deer antlers, horse manure and other remedies that promised only to make things worse. It should be no wonder that many thought the world was ending. In Paris, which lost twenty thousand of its citizens, people took over the opera house to throw an end-of-the-world masquerade ball. At the stroke of midnight, someone with a sick sense of humor arrived dressed as the grim reaper to remind the revelers that their time was near. Clearly, the party, which was reported in the United States by Poe's old critic N.P. Willis, inspired Poe to compose his tale "The Masque of the Red Death," about a prince who throws himself a similar masquerade ball during a plague.

Now that Poe was rushing to generate content to fill the *Messenger*'s next issue, which was already well behind schedule, he submitted "Shadow—A Fable," a brief tale set during an ancient plague. Still convinced his true talent might lie in comedy, Poe also contributed two comedies that will remind us why Poe is best known for his horror stories. One of these, "King Pest the First—A Tale Containing an Allegory," was a burlesque about three drunken sailors in plague times who stumble upon a death party in which the dying drink out of human skulls in a room lit by a candle inside the head of a skeleton that hangs from the ceiling. It might be an understatement to say that the story was in bad taste with memories of the cholera pandemic still fresh among millions of mourners. Robert Louis Stevenson, writing in the January 2, 1875 issue of *Academy*, opined that the author of this story could only have "ceased to be a human being."

The third tale Poe contributed to his return issue was "Loss of Breath," another dark comedy about a man who cannot breathe or speak. In a nod to Poe's time on the West Range, the character is mistaken for dead and partially dissected by a doctor. Believe it or not, some critics praised Poe's humorous takes and tried to dissuade him from wasting him time writing darker fare like "Berenice." Fortunately for generations of readers the world over, "Berenice" had sparked something in Poe. He followed it up with other horror stories including "Morella" and reprinted "Metzengerstein." But during his time at the *Messenger*, the magazine published eight of his comedies and only five of his horror stories. Also appearing were a reprint of the tragic love story "The Visionary," the first installments of his adventure novel and the beginning of a play. As he stated throughout his life, his true passion was poetry, and the thirteen poems in the *Messenger* equaled the combined total of his horror and humorous stories.

But that was just his creative work. Poe still had to supply scores of book reviews, articles and other material to fill every page of each month's issue. While that might sound dull, he demonstrated a special gift for literary criticism. In addition to having keen insights into how to construct a successful story, this literary critic also had a well-developed talent for ridiculing his rivals, as Robert Pitts and Joe Locke had already learned the hard way. Among Poe's first reviews for the *Messenger* was of *Confessions of a Poet* by Laughton Osborn. It begins, "The most remarkable feature in this production is the bad paper on which it is printed, and the typographical ingenuity with which matter barely enough for one volume has been spread over the pages of two." Poe concluded by advising the author how best to mix the gunpowder to shoot himself before producing a sequel to this dreadful volume.

Poe also took aim at the big-city northern literary establishment. When the *New York Mirror* published a glowing review of a novel that had not yet been printed, Poe discovered that the book's author worked for the *Mirror*. Poe unloaded his wrath on both the author and the magazine:

> *Well!* —*here we have it! This is* the *book*—*the book* par excellence— *the book bepuffed, beplastered, and be-*Mirrored: *the book "attributed to" Mr. Blank, and "said to be from the pen" of Mr. Asterisk: the book which has been "about to appear"—"in press"—"in progress"—"in preparation"—and "forthcoming": the book "graphic" in anticipation— "talented"a* priori—*and God knows what* in prospectu. *For the sake of every thing puffed, puffing, and puffable, let us take a peep at its contents!….Norman Leslie, gentle reader, a Tale of the Present Times, is, after all, written by nobody in the world but Theodore S. Fay, and Theodore S. Fay is nobody in the world but "one of the Editors of the New York Mirror."*

For paragraph after paragraph, Poe picked apart the book's flaws, concluding that the author's writing was "unworthy of a school-boy." Soon after the *Messenger* reached its subscribers, the *Mirror* fired back with its own insults and printed a satirical tale featuring an exaggerated version of Poe. With this, the *Southern Literary Messenger* and its young editor were thrust into the national spotlight. Of course, little of this attention was positive, and the controversies and literary feuds bothered Mr. White, who feared offending his readers. Poe, however, thrived on offending them.

Back at Mrs. Yarrington's boardinghouse, the Poes were happy, and Poe's steady, if meager, salary allowed him to provide tutors for Virginia. Neighbors described seeing the smiling, giggling Virginia strolling alongside the tall, severe Maria to the farmer's market for supplies. The walk would have taken them past the *Messenger* office at Fifteenth and Main to Seventeenth Street, where vendors sold their wares under a long, narrow building. They could pick up water for drinking or cleaning in nearby Shockoe Creek before walking back uphill to Capitol Square.

Although they may have considered themselves engaged while in Baltimore, the cousins lived together for less than a year before they became man and wife. At the time, Poe was twenty-seven, and his bride was thirteen. As previously mentioned, marrying at that age was not as common as it had once been. With improvements in living conditions in the nineteenth century, live expectancies were getting longer; there was less of a necessity to marry that early, even if the laws had yet to change. Still, one in four children did not survive until adulthood, and couples prepared for this likelihood by having more children, which increased the mother's chance of dying since about one in six women died in childbirth.

When Poe's mother married at fifteen, it was not unusual, but by the time of his wedding, more than a few people might have given the couple a second glance. Poe seemed sensitive about the age difference and may have dealt with it by telling people he was two years younger than he was. In his tale "Eleonora," in which two cousins grow up with one character's benevolent mother, Poe places their ages at fifteen and twenty. The cousins who fall in love in his story "Three Sundays in a Week" are also aged fifteen and twenty.

Poe, who already looked older than his years when he was at West Point, could not convince people he was much younger than twenty-five, but he could try to make Virginia older. He gave her age as twenty-one on their marriage bond. If self-consciousness over their age difference was one motivation for his fabrication, another, more practical reason was the fact that, before her twenty-first birthday, she would need her father's permission to marry. As a woman, Maria Clemm could not sign the marriage bond in order to give her consent. Poe had a male friend sign the bond. Poe, by the way, was not required to provide his own age on the document.

The ceremony took place three months before Virginia's fourteenth birthday in Mrs. Yarrington's parlor. Yarrington and Clemm baked the wedding cake. John Mackenzie paid for Virginia's wedding dress, which his wife sewed. Judging from the two fragments that survive in a private collection, she wore a dark blue trousseau with a busy pattern. White wedding gowns were not fashionable until four years later, when Queen Victoria wore one in her ceremony.

Minister and editor of the *Southern Religious Telegraph* Amasa Converse officiated Edgar Allan Poe's wedding to Virginia Clemm in the parlor of Mrs. Yarrington's boardinghouse on May 16, 1836. The groom was twenty-seven, and his bride was thirteen.

On the evening of May 16, 1836, the bespectacled Presbyterian minister and editor of the *Southern Religious Telegraph* Amasa Converse stood before a fireplace surmounted by a large antique mirror to officiate the ceremony. He later recalled that Maria gave her full consent to the marriage and that, as far as he could see through his thick glasses and the flickering candlelight, Virginia appeared much younger than twenty-one.

Among the few guests who squeezed into the parlor that night were Thomas White and his daughter Eliza, Poe's *Messenger* co-workers William McFarlane and John W. Fergusson, his friend Thomas W. Cleland and Virginia's playmate Jane Foster, a young girl whose small stature prevented her from seeing the ceremony. Instead, she craned her neck to glimpse its reflection in the mirror over the mantel. Foster expected the ceremony to instantly transform her companion into an adult but was surprised to see Virginia emerge neither taller nor more mature. The bride was the same as she had always been.

Jane was among the well-wishers who followed the newlyweds to their carriage and waved to them as it rolled down the street to their honeymoon in Petersburg. It would have taken at least six hours to arrive at the coffeehouse and home of Poe's friend, the magazine editor Hiram Haines, and Haines's wife, who had been one of Poe's early childhood playmates. Poe's honeymoon suite was on the second floor, facing the street. That Poe sent a letter from the *Messenger* office five days later would seem to indicate that they did not stay long in the Cockade City.

Little more is known of Poe's honeymoon. There are no surviving letters from Haines to Poe and only two from Poe to Haines. Of these two, neither mentions Poe's honeymoon, but one mentions an offer Haines made to give Virginia a pet fawn. Poe declined the offer because he could not think of a good way to transport a deer.

Even less is known about Poe's marriage. Although Maria Clemm probably kept them in separate rooms until she thought Virginia was old enough, there is no evidence that they ever shared a bed. They never had children, and Poe's later fiancée and biographer Sarah Helen Whitman, about whom you will learn in a later chapter, thought Poe and Virginia always lived as brother and sister. Ever since, different biographers proposed opposing theories to fill in the missing details. Some, like Arthur Hobson Quinn, believed there is evidence in Poe's letters and in works like his love/ghost story "Eleanora" to suggest that he loved her passionately, even if her illness left her invalid for much of their marriage. Others, like Kenneth Silverman, thought their marriage was never consummated.

The practice of Poe biographers of referring to her as his child-bride is also inaccurate because she did not stay thirteen for the duration of their marriage. The one fact of which we can be sure is that they never had children. Biographers cannot seem to agree on the reason for this. In a February 25, 2022 essay for *The Millions*, Catherine Baab-Maguira theorized that Edgar and Virginia used birth control because they realized they were too poor to care for a child.

Upon their return to Richmond, the newlyweds received congratulatory visits from his oldest friends. His life was back on track. He was married, he was happy and he was finally earning a modest living from his pen.

On Sunday afternoons, Virginia and Edgar resumed the long strolls they had enjoyed together in Baltimore. Once again, their routes took them to cemeteries. Walking just past the city's northern outskirts, they entered Shockoe Hill Cemetery, where Poe inevitably stopped at Jane Stanard's grave to tell Virginia the story of his Helen. A few paces past the Stanard plot was the resting place of John and Frances Allan. Louisa Allan, her three sons and his aunt Nancy Valentine were still living in Moldavia, but he had no contact with them.

Shortly after the wedding, Edgar and Virginia were attending a ball when Elmira saw the couple. She later related in a letter to Maria Clemm,

> *I remember seeing Edgar, & his lovely wife, very soon after they were married—I met them—I never shall forget my feelings at the time— They were indescribable, almost agonizing—"However in an instant," I remembered that I was a married woman, and banished them from me, as I would a poisonous reptile—*

Elmira apparently made enough of a scene that her husband escorted her out of the room. This, however, would not be the last she would see of Edgar, but that is a topic for another chapter.

The enterprising Maria decided to earn some extra money by opening her own boardinghouse, and to this end, Poe wrote on her behalf to the same rich uncle that Edgar's father had offended shortly after Edgar's birth. George Poe did not begrudge Edgar for his late father's behavior and contributed to the project. Edgar was also able to secure a loan of $200 from his childhood friend Robert Craig Stanard. Like many of Poe's plans, this one did not pan out. There was also a discussion of sharing Thomas White's house with his daughter Eliza, who was a published poet and friend of Edgar's. Before Virginia moved to town, rumors had spread that Edgar and Eliza, who were spotted dancing together at a ball, would have become engaged if only her father had allowed it. Regardless of the gossip, Eliza White remained Poe's friend for the rest of his life, even visiting him at his cottage in the Bronx a few months before his death.

Later that spring, when the boardinghouse scheme and the plan to share the White home failed to pan out, Edgar, Virginia and Maria moved out of Mrs. Yarrington's boardinghouse to a tenement a few blocks away on Seventh Street, where he would stay for the rest of the year. Poe was forced to borrow money to pay off the loans he had secured for furnishing the boardinghouse. He also requested $50 credit from Charles Ellis's dry-goods store. With debts pressing down on him again, Poe supplemented his salary by selling his stories and poems to the *Messenger* for about $300 per year. He also contributed works to other publications, like the Philadelphia annual *The Gift*, which carried "MS Found in a Bottle" in its 1836 installment.

Poe attracted more national attention to the *Messenger* by publishing an exposé in which he revealed that a famous chess-playing automaton, which had toured Europe and the United States for decades, was really just a scam. The supposed machine was operated by a man hiding inside of it. Poe also commenced the series *Autography*, in which he pretended to analyze celebrity autographs in order to ridicule the writers. Meanwhile, his scathing book reviews were ruffling feathers among some of the nation's most powerful authors and publishers—much to White's annoyance.

By the time Poe left the magazine in early 1837 for new opportunities in New York, White was as glad to be rid of Poe as Poe was to be out from under White's control.

VISITING MRS. YARRINGTON'S BOARDING HOUSE

As with Poe's other Richmond homes, Mrs. Yarrington's boardinghouse was demolished long ago. No plaque marks the site. A generic office building that now stands there, on the southwest corner of Twelfth and Bank Streets. All that survives of the building Poe knew are some large blocks of granite from the front steps. These are used as benches in the Poe Museum's Enchanted Garden. They are the perfect place to rest during your Poe pilgrimage to Richmond.

Visiting Hiram Haines's House

You can still visit the home in which Edgar and Virginia spent their honeymoon. It stands at 12 West Bank Street in Petersburg. About half an hour's drive on I-95 will take you to the Washington Street exit for Petersburg. Turn right off of Washington Street onto North Sycamore Street. Then turn left on Bank Street, and the house will be on the left.

Haines owned two adjoining houses on that block. He and his family lived in the one on the right, 14 West Bank Street, and his coffeehouse, in which Poe stayed, is the one on the left. While Haines' home has been altered with the removal of the upper floor, the exterior of the coffeehouse has remained much as it was during Poe's visit, with the exception of an extension on the back that covers the old carriage entrance from the alley.

After Haines's death in 1841, the building went through a succession of owners, was divided into apartments, made into a used office furniture store and eventually became a coffeehouse again. The latter was the vision of author Jeffrey Abugel, who took over the house in 2009 and set out to restore it to its original appearance. He made the first floor into a literary-themed coffee shop that served the town's best French press coffee. The restoration of the upper floors proved more difficult. After removing much of the later wallpaper and rotten floorboards, he recovered the original green paint that Edgar and Virginia saw.

He occasionally escorted guests up to the Poe room in all its decaying glory. A spiderweb pattern of cracks covered the horsehair plaster walls. The dry wood floorboards had been swept and scrubbed to remove whatever dust had not already ground its way into all the crevices. It smelled of dust with a faint touch of dried mildew. The smell of history.

Abugel celebrated Poe's birthday by holding annual seances in the room. He might even have attracted Virginia. At least, some passersby claimed to see her watching them from one of the windows. There might also be another restless spirit in residence—that of a previous owner who killed himself there.

After Abugel sold the house, its new owner converted the upper floors into apartments and the first into a salon. On a recent visit to downtown Petersburg, which now houses countless antique stores, art galleries and eclectic restaurants in its centuries-old buildings, I was standing outside the Haines House for just long enough that a woman came outside to boast about the site's history, how Poe spent his honeymoon there and how (even though the spaces have been completely renovated since Abugel's time) the original floorboards were kept for reuse elsewhere in the building. I got the feeling she had given the spiel a few times already.

When you take your Petersburg Poe pilgrimage, search the second-floor windows for a glimpse of Virginia Poe's gentle spirit staring back at you. If you gaze at the house long enough, you might also get an impromptu tour. If you are an especially big Poe fan, you can rent one of the upstairs apartments.

Chapter 12

EDGAR ALLAN POE NATIONAL HISTORIC SITE, PHILADELPHIA

In the spring of 1843, Poe and his family moved with their tortoiseshell cat Catterina into a little house in the bucolic northern suburbs of Philadelphia. The structure faced a broad green lawn where the family could sit in the cool evening breeze. The aptly named Spring Garden district was just far enough from the bustling business district for them to enjoy some fresh air and quiet. This was essential for Virginia Poe's health.

Just over a year earlier, she had been singing at her piano when everything fell apart. They had moved to the City of Brotherly Love in 1838 after a disastrous year trying to break into the magazine business in New York. The Panic of 1837 had wreaked havoc on the U.S. economy, and magazines were failing in droves. Poe could not have picked a worse time to leave the *Southern Literary Messenger*.

In New York, he had struggled to find publishers for his fiction. When a printer told him that the public preferred novels over short story collections, Poe revised the aborted *Narrative of Arthur Gordon Pym*, the first installments of which he had published in the *Southern Literary Messenger* just before he quit, and expanded it into what would become his only finished novel (if it really is finished). In the new version, Poe's narrator, Arthur Gordon Pym, informs the reader that the *Southern Literary Messenger*'s former editor Edgar Poe wrote the first two chapters for him and that the rest of the book would be taken directly from Pym's own journal. At the end of the book, a third narrator tells the reader that Pym has died and that the final pages of his journal are lost. Then this third narrator deciphers some strange symbols that Pym sees earlier in the novel. When it was finally released in book form shortly after Poe arrived in Philadelphia, the title page identified Pym as the author as if Poe intended to fool the public into thinking it was a true story. The title

The small house in the center left of this early twentieth-century photograph is the one to which Edgar Allan Poe moved with his wife and his mother-in-law in Philadelphia's Spring Garden district in 1843. They stayed for about a year. It was here that he wrote "The Gold-Bug" and "The Black Cat" and began composing "The Raven."

reads like the sort of thing readers were accustomed to seeing on the cover of nonfiction travel narratives. It reads:

The Narrative Of Arthur Gordon Pym. Of Nantucket. Comprising The Details Of A Mutiny And Atrocious Butchery On Board The American Brig Grampus, On Her Way To The South Seas, In The Month Of June, 1827. With An Account Of The Recapture Of The Vessel By The Survivers; Their Shipwreck And Subsequent Horrible Sufferings From Famine; Their Deliverance By Means Of The British Schooner Jane Guy; The Brief Cruise Of This Latter Vessel In The Antarctic Ocean; Her Capture, And The Massacre Of Her Crew Among A Group Of Islands In The Eighty-Fourth Parallel Of Southern Latitude; Together With The Incredible Adventures And Discoveries Still Farther South To Which That Distressing Calamity Gave Rise.

It is no wonder that people now simply refer to it as *The Narrative of Arthur Gordon Pym*. Some just call it *Pym*. As the full title indicates, it is a seafaring adventure featuring a mutiny, cannibalism, a plague ship, a couple massacres and the discovery of a giant being at the South Pole. It is also a tale in which little is what it seems. There are mistaken identities and a man dressing up as a murder victim's ghost. In between all the action are meticulous details of birds' nests and sea turtles.

The end result sold poorly in the United States, but in England, where bootleg copies soon began to circulate, it went through multiple editions. The main difference is that a wise British editor removed the concluding scene with the giant figure at the South Pole. Without that scene, the publishers had an easier time passing it off as a true story. In the absence of an international copyright agreement, Poe was not paid for this or any of the European reprints of his work.

The Poes were on the verge of starvation, surviving, according to their neighbor James Pedder, "on bread and molasses for weeks together." His dire circumstances drove Poe to write to the Secretary of the Navy James Kirke Paulding pleading for a job:

Could I obtain the most unimportant Clerkship in your gift—any thing, by sea or land—to relieve me from the miserable life of literary drudgery to which I now, with a breaking heart, submit, and for which neither my temper nor my abilities have fitted me, I would never again repine at any dispensation of God.

Poe had no choice but to keep selling his tales to magazines and newspapers. Along the way, he secured his second editorial post. The comedic actor William Burton had just launched *Burton's Gentlemen's Magazine* and hired Poe to edit it and write some book reviews. Before long, Poe was simultaneously editing both *Burton's* and *Alexander's Weekly Messenger* while supplying content for both.

One of the most interesting essays Poe published in *Burton's* is "The Philosophy of Furniture," in which the penniless author chastises Americans for having no taste in interior design. Not revealing to his readers that he is living in a sparsely decorated tenement with bare plaster walls, Poe instructs them on the finer points of furnishing a parlor. The red tinted-glass of the windows should be covered by crimson curtains. The carpet and upholstery should also be crimson. The walls should feature at least one gold-framed portrait of a beautiful young woman painted by his friend Thomas Sully, and no home would be complete without a copy of John Gadsby Chapman's *Lake of the Dismal Swamp*. The latter depicts rotten logs protruding from the brown waters of Lake Drummond in Virginia's infamously dreary (and haunted) swamp.

Poe's essays for *Alexander's* took on a different character. In some, he challenged his audience to send him cryptograms and puzzles to solve, and he naturally decoded them all, leading some to speculate that he had sent himself the puzzles. In another article, he reported on the murder trial of James Wood, who, having killed his family, was pleading "Not Guilty by Reason of Insanity." Poe observed that the calm manner in which Wood described his crime was the best evidence of his insanity. A couple of years later, Poe would use Wood as the inspiration for the narrator of his horror story "The Tell-Tale Heart."

In addition to dozens of Poe's essays and reviews, *Burton's* carried his best new tales, including "The Fall of the House of Usher" and "William Wilson." He also attempted to serialize a second novel, *The Journal of Julius Rodman*. This adventure yarn purported to be the true story of explorers venturing through the North American wilderness, encountering dangers like ferocious bears along the way. Burton fired his star editor before the novel's conclusion.

By this time, Burton was frustrated with Poe's scathing book reviews, which were making enemies across the country. Poe was upset with the low

This photograph taken in the 1930s depicts the kitchen in which Poe's mother-in-law, Maria Clemm, prepared meals in their house in the Spring Garden district of Philadelphia. Clemm performed the family's cooking and kept the house meticulously clean and tidy.

pay and having a comedian second-guess his literary expertise. To make matters worse, Burton had tired of owning a magazine and was attempting to sell it, an act Poe thought of as a betrayal.

Seeing White and Burton stumble through running their magazines inspired Poe to launch his own. After all, Poe reasoned, it was his own talent and sweat that had made both magazines successful. If Poe could only secure funding, he could change the American magazine industry. He got as far as publishing the prospectus for his proposed *Penn Magazine*. (Poe could never pass up a good pun.)

When Burton saw that prospectus, it was the last straw. The boss showed Poe the door. He was once again left to survive from the occasional sale of his tales to various magazines until he landed the editorship of *Graham's Lady's and Gentlemen's Magazine*. As soon as Poe got the job, he published his first detective story "The Murders in the Rue Morgue" in the April 1841 issue. In fact, it wasn't just *his* first detective story but *the* first detective story. Poe had invented a new literary genre, and it was a hit. He followed up his success with "A Descent into the Maelstrom," his new and newly revised poems, more articles about cryptography and handwriting analysis and scores of book reviews. The magazine's circulation soared, increasing at least seven times in the first year. Poe was still unsatisfied. His meager annual salary paled in comparison with the small fortune that the owner, George Rex Graham, earned for letting him do all the work.

In the meantime, Poe found time to write more books. His follow-up to *The Narrative of Arthur Gordon Pym* was a bit of hack work written for hire. *The Conchologist's First Book* is an introduction to the study of seashells. Poe contributed the introduction and rearranged the images of shells so that they began with the simplest organisms and ended with the most complex—just like today's biology textbooks do. Otherwise, the book contains information largely adapted from other books and page after page of pictures of shells. Although he contributed little to the finished work, Poe's name is prominently featured on the title page. This is because the publication was designed to be a cheaper version of professional conchologist Thomas Wyatt's more expensive textbook. When he tried to sell copies of his own book after his seashell lectures, Wyatt found it far too pricey for his attendees, so he attempted to produce a more affordable version—only to stopped by his publishers, who did not want him to undersell his own book. Wyatt's solution was to pay Poe fifty dollars to write a new introduction for a scaled-down version of Wyatt's book. The only problem, from Poe's perspective at least, was that the book sold better than anything else he would print during his lifetime. It entered its second edition a year after its initial publication. By the third edition's release, Poe had his name removed from the title page.

Shortly after *The Conchologist's First Book* went to press, Poe finally found a publisher for his first collection of short stories. He had long abandoned *The Tales of the Folio Club*. His new book would eschew the Folio Club framework and include every short story he had written to date. In order to give potential readers some sense of its diverse contents, Poe titled the two-volume set *Tales of the Grotesque and Arabesque*. The "Grotesque" stories were burlesques, which he continued to consider some of his best works. The "Arabesque" works were strange and unusual pieces. There is no mention in the title of his horror. In his preface, Poe acknowledges that some of his works might be mistaken for the popular gothic fiction of writers like Horace Walpole, Ann Radcliffe and Matthew "Monk" Lewis, but he clarifies that his work is something different than gothic literature, which he refers to as "Germanism":

> *But the truth is that, with a single exception, there is no one of these stories in which the scholar should recognise the distinctive features of that species of pseudo-horror which we are taught to call Germanic, for no better reason than that some of the secondary names of German literature have become identified with its folly. If in many of my productions terror has been the thesis, I maintain that terror is not of Germany, but of the soul,—that I have deduced this terror only from its legitimate sources, and urged it only to its legitimate results.*

As all these tales had already appeared in magazines and newspapers, the publishers thought they were taking a risk by publishing works many people had already seen. They could not offer Poe an advance, opting instead to give him a few free copies to give to friends.

This is believed to be the room in which Poe slept while living in his Spring Garden house. The furnishings are not Poe's but represent the kind of pieces he might have used during the year he spent there. The photograph was taken in the 1930s, after the home's restoration and conversion into a museum.

At least life was getting a little easier at the Poe house. Although Poe was still unable to pay off all the loans he had taken out over the years, they bought a piano and a harp for Virginia to play while Edgar accompanied her on the flute. Maria sang along. Early in the winter of the following year, they were singing by the fire when Virginia started coughing. There was something ominous about the deep chest cough that caused the whole party to fall silent and notice the crimson liquid dripping from her lips and sprinkled over the keyboard.

Poe had seen this before. They had *all* seen it before. A decade earlier, Henry had wasted away in the little rowhouse on Amity Street. Before that, Edgar had watched his foster mother, his mother and Jane Standard succumb to the disease. Now Virginia had contracted tuberculosis. In Poe's eyes, she was already dead. Within months, he had published a new tale, "Life in Death," in which a beautiful wife wastes away before his artist husband's eyes. The artist is too devoted to his art to notice her suffering. The tale, now known as "The Oval Portrait," may express Poe's guilt over being too committed to his literary dreams to provide Virginia the attention she deserved.

The following month, he published "The Masque of the Red Death," a tale about the impossibility of escaping death. The next major poem he published was "The Conqueror Worm," which depicts humans as powerless pawns in the face of their ruler, Death.

In the aftermath of Virginia's illness, Poe quit *Graham's Magazine* and attempted to secure an appointment to a customshouse job in the Tyler administration. John Tyler, who had assumed the presidency the previous year after the death of William Henry Harrison, was a Virginian, and Poe was acquainted with his son Robert, whom Poe thought might be able to assist him.

While he waited to months for his chance to meet the president, Poe resumed his efforts to launch his journal. To this end, he made an unsuccessful attempt to purchase the *Southern Literary Messenger*'s subscriber list. Poe had some cause for hope when he reached an agreement with newspaper publisher Thomas C. Clarke to print the magazine under its new name, *The Stylus*. Once again, the process stalled.

With plans for the new magazine in the works, Poe attempted to solve the recent murder of the popular New York cigar store clerk Mary Cecelia Rogers. He sold his solution, in the guise of the serialized tale "The Mystery of Marie Roget," to *Snowden's Lady's Companion* in New York. After the first two installments set up all the clues that would lead to his solution in the final one,

The earliest known daguerreotype of Poe, this image was captured in early 1843, shortly before he moved into the Spring Garden house. It is also the only photograph to show him without his famous mustache. The original daguerreotype has been missing for over a century.

a witness was "accidentally" shot by one of her sons. On her deathbed, the widow Henrietta Loss admitted that Rogers had died during an underground abortion carried out in her tavern. Poe, who previously believed that Rogers had been strangled by a jealous lover, postponed the publication of the final installment to rewrite his ending. It turned out that not only did the abortion theory not correlate with the facts recorded in Rogers's autopsy but also that the confession probably never happened.

In need of cash before he could rewrite the last installment, Poe jotted down what would one day be his most popular story. Recalling the case of family annihilator James Wood, Poe crafted his masterpiece "The Tell-Tale Heart." Then he sent it to the *Boston Miscellany*, which promptly rejected it. His friend James Russell Lowell, however, agreed to give Poe ten dollars for the piece and published it in the first issue of his new magazine, *The Pioneer*.

Unemployed and with no prospects for the future, Poe declared bankruptcy before the end of the year. In March 1843, his appointment to meet John Tyler was set. The poet got as far as traveling to Washington, D.C., where someone persuaded him to take a drink of port wine at a party. He was soon so drunk that his friends caught him wearing his coat inside-out and had to stop him from meeting the president in that condition.

Shortly after his return to Philadelphia, Poe moved with his dying wife and his mother-in-law into the Spring Garden house. They rented it from a plumber named William M. Alburger, who was lenient about Poe's habitually late payments. Even in the suburbs, the place was dwarfed by the mansions of their Quaker neighbors, but it was infinitely better than some of the lean-tos they had occupied before he got the job at Burton's. Although the house was three stories tall, each floor was barely big enough to hold more than one or two rooms.

Writing for the April 1869 issue of *Onward*, Poe's friend, the novelist Mayne Reid, recalled that the home was "a lean-to of three rooms, (there may have been a garret with a closet,) of painted plank construction, supported against the gable of the more pretentious dwelling."

Reid continued,

> *In this humble domicile I can say, that I have spent some of the pleasantest hours of my life—certainly some of the most intellectual. They were passed in the company of the poet himself, and his wife—a lady angelically beautiful in person and not less beautiful in spirit. No one who remembers that dark-eyed, dark-haired daughter of Virginia—her own name, if I rightly remember—her grace, her facial beauty, her demeanor, so modest as*

This image shows the parlor of Poe's Spring Garden house in the 1930s, after it was restored and redecorated by Poe collector Richard Gimbel. The furniture seen here is probably too ornate and too plentiful to be historically accurate. Poe's visitors described the parlor as sparsely and simply furnished.

to be remarkable—no one who has ever spent an hour in her company but will endorse what I have above said. I remember how we, the friends of the poet, used to talk of her high qualities. And when we talked of her beauty, I well knew that the rose-tint upon her cheek was too bright, too pure to be of Earth. It was consumption's color—that sadly beautiful light that beckons to an early tomb.

In the little lean-to, besides the poet and his interesting wife, there was but one other dweller. This was a woman of middle age, and almost masculine aspect. She had the size and figure of a man, with a countenance that, at first sight, seemed scarce feminine. A stranger would have been incredulous—surprised, as I was, when introduced to her as the mother of that angelic creature who had accepted Edgar Poe as the partner of her life.

When her health permitted her to meet visitors, she was cheerful and playful. Clarke's daughter Anne E.C. Clarke recalled singing "the old song of Gaffer-Poe" to entertain her.

When the Poes rented the house, it was fairly new, its interior walls still covered in fresh horsehair plaster. Maria Clemm kept the place meticulously clean, regularly washing the pristine walls. Visitors to Poe's house describe it as being clean and well-ordered but sparsely decorated, a far cry from the room he envisioned in "The Philosophy of Furniture." His soon-to-be enemy Rufus Griswold recalled in his 1850 memoir of the author,

I was impressed by the singular neatness and the air of refinement in his home. It was in a small house, in one of the pleasant and silent neighborhoods far from the centre of the town, and though slightly and cheaply furnished, everything in it was so tasteful and so fitly disposed that it seemed altogether suitable for a man of genius.

According to Reid,

[Clemm] was also the messenger to the market; from it bringing back, not the "delicacies of the season," but only such commodities as were called for by the dire exigencies of hunger.

And yet, were there some delicacies. I shall never forget how, when peaches were in season and cheap, a pottle of these, the choicest gifts of Pomona, were divested of their skins by the delicate fingers of the poet's wife, and left to the "melting mood," to be amalgamated with Spring Garden cream and crystallized sugar, and then set before such guests as came in by chance.

Between his efforts to launch his magazine, planning new books, supplying content for multiple magazines and trying to solve a murder mystery, Poe spent most of his day holed up in his second-floor bedroom over his writing desk. Despite his diligent efforts, Poe was still struggling to keep a roof above their heads. To make matters worse, Clarke had withdrawn his support for *The Stylus*.

Just when his outlook was at its most bleak, Poe read that the *Dollar Newspaper* was offering a one-hundred-dollar prize for the best short story. That was a year's rent.

For this one, he revisited his detective stories and added one of his beloved cryptograms. "The Gold-Bug" features an eccentric code-breaking entomologist named Legrand and his side-kick Jupiter, a manumitted former slave. When Legrand stumbles upon a message written in invisible ink, he heats the paper to reveal an encrypted message that will lead them to Captain Kidd's buried treasure. Poe later revealed that he wrote the story to be a popular favorite and that he knew the public would love a story about people who use their wits to discover fabulous riches. Poe would know. He had spent his entire career chasing after that dream. For now, he would have to settle for just enough to provide the necessities of life for his ailing wife and devoted mother-in-law.

"The Gold-Bug" was certain to win the prize. The only problem was that he had already sold it to *Graham's Magazine* for fifty dollars. Poe scrambled to write some content he could trade to George Graham for the story. Then he submitted his tale to the contest.

Not only did Poe win the first prize, but the papers could not stop praising his tale as well. The *Dollar Newspaper* ran out of copies of the issues containing Poe's story and had to reprint them to meet demand. Once "The Gold-Bug" was in print, other papers across the country reprinted it. By Poe's estimate, its circulation, between all the different publications that carried it, was at least 300,000 copies. It was not long before the story was adapted into a stage play. In the absence of today's copyright protections, Poe received nothing for all the reprints, the dramatization or the foreign reprints.

That left him to try another scheme. From his years of experience in the magazine business, Poe may have come to believe that the future of American literary was "magazine-ward." Due to their expense, books were naturally restricted to a wealthy readership, but everyone could afford a newspaper or magazine. The only way to reach a mass audience was to reach the audience through mass-produced periodicals.

After the failure of his last collection of short stories, Poe decided a cheaper book, containing only two of his stories at a time, would finally reach the mass audience he deserved. The first issue of the proposed series, *The Prose Romances of Edgar A. Poe*, featured "The Murders in the Rue Morgue" and "The Man That Was Used Up." Unfortunately, the first number was also the last.

About this time, Poe may have attempted to study law, but if he did, the documentation has not been located. This would have been just another failed attempt to escape the life of literature, but it only forced him back to his desk, where he soon produced and sold the horror tale "The Black Cat" to the *Saturday Evening Post* for twenty dollars.

He was also at work on a new poem, probably the best thing he had ever written, but when he showed it to the editors of *Graham's*, they ridiculed this bizarre composition about a man who attempts to carry on a conversation with a raven who knows only a single word. What Poe had intended to evoke melancholy from his audience must have sounded laughable to the editors if, even though they refused to publish it, they sent him a donation of fifteen dollars to help him pay the rent.

Poe would spend at least another year fine-tuning the poem that was to eventually become "The Raven." The early version he attempted to sell to *Graham's* does not survive. Fortunately, Poe's revisions made it into the most popular poem in American literature, the only poem most adults can remember having read.

Meanwhile Poe stationed himself at his desk all day and continued to generate new content for the press. By night, he delivered sold-out lectures about American poetry. Virginia's health improved enough for her to spend more time outdoors, tending to the flowerbeds.

A young neighbor of the Poes later recalled,

> *Twice a day, on my way to and from school…I had to pass their house, and in summer time often saw them. In the mornings Mrs. Clemm and her daughter would be generally watering the flowers, which they had in a bed under the windows. They seemed always cheerful and happy, and I could hear Mrs. Poe's laugh before I turned the corner. Mrs. Clemm was always busy. I have seen her of mornings clearing the front yard, washing the windows and the stoop, and even white-washing the palings. You would notice how clean and orderly everything looked. She rented out her front room to lodgers, and used the middle room, next to the kitchen, for their own living room or parlor. They must have slept under the roof.*

Even if they were taking in boarders to help pay the bills, they were still having trouble making the rent. As another young neighbor, Lydia Hart Garrigues, later recounted,

> *He, his wife and Mrs. Clemm, kept to themselves. They had the reputation of being very reserved—we thought because of their poverty and his great want of success. We knew he did not pay his rent to Mr. Alburger, who, however, was not disposed to cause him distress.*

Clemm continued to manage the family's money and to run errands. She, more than anyone, understood how desperate their situation had become. In early 1844, Poe borrowed a volume of the *Southern Literary Messenger* from his friend Henry Hirst, who had borrowed it from the private library of the Philadelphia scholar William Duane. When Poe was done with the volume, he asked Clemm to return it to Hirst. She sold it to a bookseller instead.

When Duane asked him to return the book, Poe assured him that Clemm had left it at Hirst's office. Eventually, a friend of Duane's found the volume in a Richmond bookstore. Since Duane had written his name on the title page, it was obviously his book. Duane wrote back to Poe to accuse him of having stolen the book. Unwilling to accept that Clemm had deceived him, Poe blamed Hirst. On January 28, 1845, Poe wrote to Duane, "To the person of whom I borrowed the book, or rather who insisted upon forcing it on me, I have sufficient reason to believe that it was returned. Settle your difficulties with him, and insult me with no more of your communications."

The whole affair made Poe more enemies and left him looking like a liar and a thief. His relationships with some of Philadelphia's literary lions were beginning to deteriorate, and his chances of securing funding to launch *The Stylus* were looking grim. It was time to search for new opportunities and new funding streams in the nation's most populous city—New York. After about a year in the Spring Garden home, Edgar and Virginia caught the train to Manhattan to find a boardinghouse. This closed the chapter on Poe's extremely productive Philadelphia period. It was in that city that Poe wrote what would become most of his best-known tales.

THE EDGAR ALLAN POE NATIONAL HISTORIC SITE AFTER POE

The Poe house in Philadelphia passed through a succession of owners before Richard Gimbel purchased it. Born in 1898, Gimbel was the grandson of the founder of Gimbels department stores. He worked for the family business and could have lived a successful, safe and boring life, but he had other plans. He served on the 310th Field Artillery Regiment during World War I, attaining the rank of first lieutenant. After studying in Europe, he graduated with honors from Yale before moving to Philadelphia to oversee the construction of a Gimbels store.

He soon became interested in rare book collecting, with an emphasis on Poe. Learning of the Poe Museum in Richmond, he wrote them to ask for a catalogue of all their antiquarian books. Before long, he was competing with the museum for newly available artifacts. With his deep pockets, Gimbel was able to win a hoard of manuscripts, first editions and first printings at auction.

A few years later, he decided to start an Edgar Allan Poe Club in Philadelphia. In 1934, he celebrated Poe's 125th birthday with a dinner for 1,600 of Poe's admirers and by opening the Poe House in Spring Garden to the public. One of the house's rooms was devoted to displaying his Poe collection, which newspaper reports at the time valued at $500,000—not bad in today's money but astounding in 1934 dollars. He filled the other rooms with antique furniture from Poe's time. Although he could acquire actual Poe furnishings, he researched the types of chairs and tables the Poe family could have owned and attempted to decorate the home as Poe would have known it.

A year later, he stepped down as vice president of Gimbels to launch a rival store in Miami. When the United States entered World War II, he served as a pilot in the Eighth Air Force, rising to the rank of colonel. After the war, he taught air science and tactics at Yale, where he eventually became the curator of his 100,000-volume collection of aeronautical books.

Gimbel left both his Poe house and his Poe collection to the City of Philadelphia to operate it after his death. The Free Library took the collection, but the house, shorn of its original Poeana, deteriorated over the years until the National Park Service stepped in to restore it and keep it open to the public as the Edgar Allan Poe National Historic Site.

Visiting the Edgar Allan Poe National Historic Site

Poe's last surviving Philadelphia home is administered by the National Park Service, so it is actually part of Independence National Historical Park, a district that also includes Independence Hall, the Liberty Bell, the Tomb of the Unknown Revolutionary War Soldier, the Second Bank of the United States and several other sites that mostly relate to the American Revolution. If you intend to visit those historic sites, you will find that the Poe Site is not within walking distance.

The Poe site sits north of Old City just past Seventh and Spring Garden at 352 North Seventh Street. There are bus stops nearby at Seventh and Green Streets and at Seventh and Spring Garden Streets. You can drive, but you will not find any off-street parking. Be sure to check their website or call ahead to make sure it will be open during your visit.

The helpful park rangers will send you through the house on a self-guided tour. Rather than furnishing the house with period furniture that has no connection to Poe, the site has opted to install large banners with renderings of what furniture might have been in each room. Otherwise, the house's interior is mostly three floors of bare walls and floors, but that makes visitors pay even closer attention, scanning every corner for some slight trace of the Poes' presence, for something they might have seen or left behind. Climbing those narrow steps and standing in those empty rooms is like exploring an archaeological site—especially if you are lucky enough to go alone.

Guests enter into the first-floor parlor, just as they did in Poe's day. This is where he would have entertained his friends and potential financial backers. It may have echoed with the music of Virginia Poe's piano. Next to this room is the kitchen, where Maria Clemm prepared meals on the wood stove.

The second-floor bedroom was probably Poe's bedroom and where he did most of his writing. The third-floor bedrooms likely belonged to his wife and mother-in-law. Once you have spent a while in each of these spaces, head down the rickety wooden steps to everybody's favorite room—the basement. On one end, a structure called a false chimney has been broken away to reveal a perfect place for hiding a corpse. It is exactly the sort of false chimney the narrator of Poe's tale "The Black Cat" used to dispose of his wife's body. This has led some people to believe that Poe was inspired to write that story by living in this house. Poe published the story in August 1843, four months after moving into the Spring Garden house, so it is entirely possible that he wrote it there. Recalling the event forty years later, Poe's friend Felix

O.C. Darely said Poe read the story to him in late 1842, which would mean that Poe composed "The Black Cat" before moving to Spring Garden. Of course, Darely *could* have misremembered the exact date. It certainly would be quite a coincidence if Poe moved into a house with a false chimney *after* having described it in his story.

The house in which the Poes lived is attached to two other buildings, so the site converted the non-Poe spaces into a gift shop, an introductory exhibit, an orientation video screening room and a reading room with red carpet, red furniture, red curtains and a gold-framed painting of a woman by Thomas Sully. If that sounds familiar, it is because this is a re-creation of Poe's essay "The Philosophy of Furniture."

If you would like to see Richard Gimbel's Poeana collection, you can find it at the Free Library of Philadelphia's Rare Book Department. In addition to Poe's manuscripts for "The Murders in the Rue Morgue" and "Annabel Lee," a rare daguerreotype of Poe and one of twelve known copies of Poe's first book, *Tamerlane*, they have Charles Dickens's stuffed pet raven Grip. There is even a legend (probably started by Dickens fans) that Grip inspired Poe to write "The Raven." Call or check their website for information on their free daily tours of the collection.

Chapter 13
BRENNEN FARMHOUSE, NEW YORK

Around three o'clock in the afternoon, Edgar and Virginia arrived at the Walnut Street Wharf in the pouring rain. Edgar left her on the steamboat while he searched for an umbrella and a room. After finding both, he picked up Virginia in a hack and took her to a boardinghouse on Greenwich Street, near Cedar.

The next morning after breakfast, he reported back to Maria Clemm in Philadelphia. In this April 7, 1844 letter, Poe reassured Muddy that "Sissy coughed none at all" during the trip and hardly at all since, that her night sweats were gone and that she "had a hearty cry" the previous night because she missed Muddy and Catterina.

In an effort to convince her that this trip would turn out better than his Washington, D.C. visit, Poe informed Muddy, "I feel in excellent spirits & haven't drank a drop—so that I hope so [on] to get out of trouble." As soon as he could come up with the money, he would send for her to join them.

Most of the letter was devoted to loving descriptions of the food he ate at the boardinghouse:

> *I wish Kate could see it—she would faint. Last night, for supper, we had the nicest tea you ever drank, strong & hot—wheat bread & rye bread—cheese—tea-cakes (elegant) a great dish (2 dishes) of elegant ham, and 2 of cold veal piled up like a mountain and large slices—3 dishes of the cakes and, and every thing in the greatest profusion. No fear of starving here....For breakfast we had excellent-flavored [coffee], hot & strong—*

not very clear & no great deal of cream—veal cutlets, elegant ham & eggs & nice bread and butter. I never sat down to a more plentiful or a nicer breakfast. I wish you could have seen the eggs—and the great dishes of meat. I ate the first hearty breakfast I have eaten since I left our little home.

A few days later, he sold an article to the *Sun*, a widely read penny paper—one of a new class of mass-produced newspapers printed on cheap paper and sold for one cent per issue. His contribution appeared in an April 13 broadside under a flashy headline:

ASTOUNDING NEWS! BY EXPRESS VIA NORFOLK! THE ATLANTIC CROSSED IN THREE DAYS! SIGNAL TRIUMPH OF MR. MONCK MASON'S FLYING MACHINE!!! Arrival at Sullivan's Island, near Charleston, S. C., of Mr. Mason, Mr. Robert Holland, Mr. Henson, Mr. Harrison Ainsworth, and four others, in the STEERING BALLOON "VICTORIA," AFTER A PASSAGE OF SEVENTY-FIVE HOURS FROM LAND TO LAND. FULL PARTICULARS OF THE VOYAGE!!!

New Yorkers snatched up every copy of the paper to learn how the famous Irish balloonist Thomas Monck Mason had crossed the Atlantic. It was already well-known that Mason had flown a balloon for a record-setting five hundred miles from London to Weilburg in an astonishing eighteen hours. Now he had apparently crossed the ocean in a mere seventy-five hours—a fraction of the three weeks it took to make the trip by ship.

The May 25 issue of Pennsylvania's *Columbia Spy* reported:

On the morning (Saturday) of [the balloon trip's] *announcement, the whole square surrounding the "Sun" building was literally besieged, blocked up — ingress and egress being alike impossible, from a period soon after sunrise until about two o'clock P.M....I never witnessed more intense excitement to get possession of a newspaper. As soon as the few first copies made their way into the streets, they were bought up, at almost any price, from the news-boys, who made a profitable speculation beyond doubt. I saw a half-dollar given, in one instance, for a single paper, and a shilling [12½ cents] was a frequent price. I tried, in vain, during the whole day, to get possession of a copy....Of course there was great discrepancy of opinion as regards the authenticity of the story; but I observed that the more intelligent believed, while the rabble, for the most part, rejected the whole with disdain.*

The *Columbia Spy*'s version of events should be taken with a grain of salt because Poe wrote it, so it was probably only slightly more trustworthy than his article about the balloon trip, which was, of course, a hoax. It was soon retitled "The Balloon-Hoax." The truth is that almost no one seems to have fallen for Poe's hoax, especially since the *Sun* had risen to fame almost a decade earlier by publishing a series of similar articles by Richard Adams Locke, who claimed that an astronomer's telescope had revealed bat-men living on the moon. In this case, the public actually believed him, at least for a while, but by Poe's time, New Yorkers exposed to a steady supply of hoaxes were a bit less likely to believe everything they read in the paper.

This did not deter Poe from publishing similar hoaxes—and claiming that everyone believed them. A few months later, the *Columbian Magazine* published his article "Mesmeric Revelation," which purports to be the account of a man mesmerized at the moment of death to allow him to communicate with the living from the other side.

In addition to publishing articles in the *Columbia Spy*, Poe was selling work to *Graham's Magazine*, the *Gift* and the *Opal*. A month after his arrival in New York, he was able to bring Maria Clemm up to live with him and Virginia. For the sake of Virginia's health, Poe found the family accommodations on the top floor of a two-story Dutch-style farmhouse belonging to Patrick and Mary Brennen in the area of present-day Eighty-Fourth Street near Broadway. When Poe first approached Mrs. Brennen, she had ten children and was not interested in taking in boarders, but something about the way he pleaded for the sake of his wife's health won her over.

When Poe lived there, the house was perched on a hill in the countryside a few miles outside of the city. From his window, Poe could see beyond the Hudson River to the Palisades in the distance. The place was surrounded by a grove of trees, and a spring provided plentiful and clean drinking water.

The trio had a simple large room with a fireplace adorned by an ornate mantel painted black. The sole decorations were some engravings of military scenes and a small plaster bust of Athena. A few pieces of furniture and some bookshelves completed the room. Poe kept his writing desk, littered with books and paper, next to the window overlooking the river. Edgar, Sissy and Muddy kept to themselves, taking their meals in their room rather than eating downstairs with the Brennens. At night, Maria slept in a room downstairs while Edgar, Virginia and Catterina stayed upstairs.

When he wasn't writing, Poe strolled through the fields and forests and sat along the banks of the Hudson. In the summer, he enjoyed swimming

In 1844, Poe and his family moved into the top floor of this farmhouse just outside New York City. While there, he finished composing "The Raven"—the poem that would make him famous. The house has since been demolished, but the mantel from his room has been saved and is owned by Columbia University.

in a nearby watering hole. Sometimes, when her health permitted, Virginia joined him for some fresh air and sunshine, clapping and giggling in delight while he performed for her in the water.

His favorite spot was an enormous rock named Mount Tom, on which he could sit for hours, lost in thought. Sometimes he and Virginia would stay there until dark, and Mr. Brennen had to go remind him to come home.

Between his assignments for the *Columbia Spy* and other periodicals, Poe continued to revise the poem he had begun in the Spring Garden house. The Brennens' oldest daughter, the fifteen-year-old Martha Susannah, took a special interest in her mother's tenants. Accompanied by her bulldog Tiger and terrier Askine, Martha followed them on afternoon strolls to Mount Tom, carrying parasols and wraps for Virginia and Maria. Afterward, she would sit on the floor next to Poe's writing desk while he worked. As he dropped his papers face-down on the floor, she picked them up, carefully arranging them.

One night, a violent tempest swept across the countryside, pounding the roof and threatening to level the house. The next morning, according to

Martha, Poe finally completed the poem. Thereafter, the family referred to that upstairs room as the Raven Room.

Poe tried again to find a publisher for "The Raven." This time, a journal devoted to Whig Party politics, the *American Review*, paid him about fifteen dollars and printed it in the February 1845 issue, which probably hit newsstands in the middle of January. The poem appeared under the pseudonym Quarles. Although this was standard practice for the magazine, one friend of Poe's suggested that Poe published it anonymously because he worried it might be so bad that it would ruin his reputation if he printed it under his own name.

If that is true, he had no need to fear. As soon as the *American Review* typeset "The Raven," the *Evening Mirror* reprinted it with Poe's name under the title. In a prefatory comment, the editor N.P. Willis (the same critic who had previously described burning "Al Aaraaf" in the fireplace) proclaimed that Poe's latest composition would "stick to the memory of everyone who

The same month "The Raven" debuted in the *American Review*, *Graham's Magazine* printed this portrait of Poe to accompany an article about his life and work. The engravers Thomas B. Welch and Adam B. Walter copied the image from a watercolor of Poe by A.C. Smith. Few who knew Poe well thought it bore any resemblance to the poet.

reads it." Willis was right. Papers and magazines across the country reprinted it, making Poe a celebrity overnight. It did not hurt that, by coincidence, *Graham's Magazine* carried a full-page portrait of Poe followed by a long and flattering article about him in its February 1845 issue.

Already experienced in delivering lectures about poets and poetry, Poe now started recited his greatest hit to sold-out crowds at concert halls and lyceums on the East Coast. Afterward, children recognized the author, crying out "Nevermore! Nevermore!" Poe could not attend the theater without the actors calling "Nevermore!" from the stage.

Poe also found steady employment as an assistant editor at the *Mirror*, where he and N.P. Willis developed a lasting friendship. It was a good start to a year that would see Poe release new collections of his tales and poems and take over ownership of his own literary magazine, the *Broadway Journal*. His new job required him to move Virginia, Maria and Catterina into the city with him. They lived in a series of boardinghouses before settling into one on Amity Street in Greenwich Village in October.

THE BRENNEN FARMHOUSE AFTER POE

New York City has swallowed up the countryside that Poe and the Brennens once knew. The farmhouse eventually fell for the sake of progress, but all is not lost. In 1922, the New York Shakespeare Society placed a plaque on a building near the Brennen farmhouse site to remind passersby that America's most popular poem was written near that spot. If that is not enough, you can still find a piece of the house if you know where to look.

In 1888, shortly before the farmhouse was demolished, William Hemstreet decided that, if he couldn't save the house, he would at least take home a souvenir from the room in which Poe composed "The Raven." Rather than carry home a brick or a shingle, he chose to lug a large wooden mantel down the stairs and back home to Brooklyn with him. One can only imagine how he explained this souvenir to his carriage driver.

For the next two decades, he displayed the Raven mantel in his home library. Then he decided to offer the piece to an institution that would agree to preserve the relic and keep it on public display. The morning the *New York Times* printed his offer of what they referred to as the Raven Mantel, he started getting calls from organizations eager to give it a home. Poe's alma mater in Charlottesville vied for the Raven Mantel, but it was Columbia

University that finally won the prize when university president Nicholas M. Butler personally assured Hemstreet that the relic would be installed in a place of honor and cared for to the best of the university's ability. At the beginning of 1908, Hemstreet officially donated the Raven Mantel to Columbia University, which installed it in the Low Library, where it remained for sixty-six years. Then the Raven Mantel flew over to the Butler Library, where it "still is sitting" in a room on the sixth floor in the Rare Book and Manuscript Library.

VISITING THE BRENNEN FARMHOUSE MANTEL AND SITE

You will need to make an appointment to see the Raven Mantel and have a good reason to visit, so check their website for more information before you go. They have an entire "Frequently Asked Questions" page devoted to how

This bronze plaque placed near the corner of Eighty-Fourth Street and Broadway in New York by the New York Shakespeare Society might mark the location of the house in which Poe completed "The Raven." Just in case it is in the wrong place, there is a second plaque attached to a building across the street.

to make an appointment. The Rare Book and Manuscript Library also owns an important daguerreotype of Poe and some choice manuscripts—including one for "Annabel Lee." (I know I told you there was one in Philadelphia, but there is also one in New York.)

If getting into the Butler Library proves too difficult, you can visit the site of the Brennen farmhouse at Eighty-Fourth Street and Broadway, but that is easier said than done. The New York Shakespeare Society installed its plaque on a building on the west side of Broadway, but it might be in the wrong place. Some historians believe the house was actually on the east side of Broadway, so they placed a second plaque across the street, on the wall of the Eagle Court Apartment Building at 215 West Eighty-Fourth Street. Just in case neither of those plaques marks the spot, the city designated the section of Eighty-Fourth Street between Broadway and Riverside Drive Edgar Allan Poe Street. We can only hope that Poe's home was somewhere on the street named after him.

If you follow Edgar Allan Poe Street for a few blocks and cross Riverside Drive, you just might see a massive rock rising up from the trees and brush in a little park. That's Mount Tom. To get the full Poe experience, pay a visit to the place where Poe used to sit for hours, rehearsing his poetry and contemplating how to finish "The Raven."

Chapter 14

POE'S LAST MANHATTAN RESIDENCE, NEW YORK

*S*hortly after Poe moved with his family to Greenwich Village, Anne Charlotte Lynch, host of a popular weekly literary soiree, added Poe to her guest list. Virginia rarely left the house anymore but encouraged him to attend because she believed that socializing with the city's literati would keep him in good spirits and out of trouble. She was wrong.

Among the new friends he made was the beloved poet Frances Sargent Osgood, the wife of the portraitist Samuel S. Osgood. Bubbly and flirtatious, Osgood had already attracted the attention of the dour editor and anthologist Rufus Wilmot Griswold, who already knew—and disliked—Poe from their days in Philadelphia. Poe had been ridiculing Griswold and criticizing his book *The Poets and Poetry of America* in print and on the lecture circuit for years. Osgood thought enough of Griswold to dedicate her most recent book of poetry to him. That was about to change now that Poe was a regular guest at Lynch's soirees.

Poe and Osgood began addressing mildly flirtatious poetry to each other. Most of Poe's poems for her, like "To Frances" and "To F—— S—— O——," were actually older poems that had previously been addressed to other women before he rededicated them to her and changed their titles. When both of these poems appeared in his 1845 collection *The Raven and Other Poems*, it was obvious to everyone in the New York literary scene who "F—— S—— O——" was, and rumors began to circulate.

This did not seem to bother either Virginia or Samuel Osgood, who painted Poe's portrait at this time. Virginia befriended Frances and welcomed her into their home. Consequently, Frances Osgood provides an inside look at the Amity Street home in an article she wrote immediately after Poe's death for the December 8, 1849 issue of *Saroni's Musical Times*.

According to Osgood, "It was in his own simple yet poetical home that, to me, the character of Edgar Poe appeared in its most beautiful light."

She found the author of "The Raven" to be "playful, affectionate, witty, alternately docile and wayward as a petted child—for his young, gentle and idolized wife, and for all who came, he had even in the midst of his most harassing literary duties, a kind word, a pleasant smile, a graceful and courteous attention."

The only other reference she made to the interior of the Amity Street was the mention of a "romantic picture of his loved and lost Lenore" hanging above his writing desk. Elsewhere in the article, Osgood states that Virginia had been the inspiration for his poem "Annabel Lee," so it is possible that the "lost Lenore" (a reference to "The Raven") is also Virginia, who was "lost" to tuberculosis before Osgood wrote the essay. If Virginia is Lenore, then the question remains as to what portrait of her could possibly have hung over his writing desk. The only fully authenticated portrait of her is the watercolor made after her death, well after the Poes moved out of the Amity Street house.

Since the watercolor depicts her postmortem, it hardly fits the description of a "romantic" picture, which likely means an image of a person dressed in archaic or exotic clothing or standing in an idealized or fanciful landscape. It could be one of two oil paintings said to represent Virginia. The one in a Texas private collection depicts a young woman picking flowers. Its dubious provenance suggests that the artist Thomas Sully gave it to the British painter Joseph Thomas Scott around 1870. The fact that it did not leave Sully's studio until then seems to rule out the possibility that it could have belonged to the Poe family.

The second oil painting belonged to Eliza Rebecca Herring's direct descendant Antoinette Smith Suiter, who intended it to go to the Poe Museum. While the portrait resembles the postmortem painting of Virginia Poe, some Poe scholars are skeptical of its authenticity.

Another possibility is that the portrait of Lenore was merely a mass-produced print of a woman that reminded him of one of the Sully portraits he described in "The Philosophy of Furniture." A stylistically similar print is said to have hung in the house in which the Poes lived after they left Amity Street.

Osgood remembered a lighthearted scene in the Amity Street house. Edgar and Virginia had invited her to see his new manuscripts for a series of essays about New York's writers. He had written each author's essay on a different piece of paper, which was cut into a long, narrow strip and rolled up like a scroll. He told Frances that the longest scrolls were devoted to his favorite authors. With Virginia's help, he unrolled one scroll after another until they came to one that stretched out across the room, Virginia giggling in delight as she ran to the opposite wall with her end of the paper. When Frances asked who the subject of that essay was, Edgar replied, "Hear her! Just as if her little vain heart didn't tell her it's herself!"

This portrait is said to depict Edgar Allan Poe's wife and cousin Virginia Clemm, but not enough of its provenance is known to fully authenticate it.

Those times did not last.

Frances was not the only woman interested in Poe. Another attendee of Lynch's soirees, the poet Elizabeth Ellet, sent Poe a letter with a postscript, written in German, inviting him to her apartment that evening. After he failed to appear, she sent another letter, asking if he could read German. Unable to take a hint, Ellet made a nuisance of herself by occasionally dropping by his house. On one such visit, she claimed that she spotted a letter from Frances to Edgar lying open on a table. Since the wax seal had been broken, she thought she had every right to read his mail. What she saw horrified her. At least, we will have to take her word for that because she refused to say exactly what it said, other than hinting that it contained evidence of an adulterous affair and something worse. This is all it took to start the rumor mill spinning. There were suggestions that Poe could have fathered Osgood's baby Fannie Fay. There was speculation about a trip Edgar and Frances had made to Providence that summer without their spouses. (More about that in the next chapter!)

Stirred up by Ellet's righteous indignation, Lynch and a party of her friends arrived at Poe's house to demand he return every letter Frances had ever sent him. Poe barked back that he had already bundled up all the letters and left them at her door. It should have ended there, but Poe is almost always his own worst enemy. Instead of slamming the door on Lynch's mob, he felt the need to get himself into more trouble. He told them that Mrs. Ellet had better worry about the things she had sent him.

With that statement, he made himself a lifelong enemy of Ellet. Since her husband was living in South Carolina, she sent her brother to the Amity Street house to call him a liar and demand that Poe retract his statement.

Poe headed to his acquaintance Thomas Dunn English to borrow a gun, either to defend himself or to challenge Ellet's brother to a duel. When English refused, fists started flying. According to English, he left Poe bloody and hiding under a couch. Poe told everyone the opposite version of events.

Edgar's reputation was ruined, and he was taken off Lynch's guest list and no longer welcome in polite society. As beloved as she was, Frances was still tormented by gossip and innuendo. Virginia, too, was so traumatized by Ellet's actions that she referred to the busybody as her "murderer."

Poe retaliated by writing a series of articles for Philadelphia's *Godey's Lady's Book*, the most popular magazine in the United States. In *The Literati of New York City*, Poe listed the authors he had met in the city, complementing some and ridiculing others. The series was a smash hit, with readers clamoring for every issue of *Godey's* that promised to carry an installment. So great was the demand that *Godey's* reprinted the first installment in the next issue. Naturally, some of the writers in Lynch's circle were furious, especially Thomas Dunn English.

In the third installment of *The Literati*, published in the July 1846 issue of *Godey's*, Poe fired off a few of his choicest insults at his old sparring partner:

> *The inexcusable sin of Mr. E. is imitation—if this be not too mild a term. Barry Cornwall and others of the bizarre school are his especial favorites. He has taken, too, most unwarrantable liberties, in the way of downright plagiarism, from a Philadelphian poet whose high merits have not been properly appreciated— Mr. Henry B. Hirst....I place Mr. English, however, on my list of New York literati, not on account of his poetry, (which I presume he is not weak enough to estimate very highly,) but on the score of his having edited for several months, "with the aid of numerous collaborators," a monthly magazine called "The Aristidean."....No spectacle can be more pitiable than that of a man without the commonest school education busying himself in attempts to instruct mankind on topics of polite literature. The absurdity in such*

cases does not lie merely in the ignorance displayed by the would-be instructor, but in the transparency of the shifts by which he endeavours to keep this ignorance concealed....I make these remarks in no spirit of unkindness. Mr. E. is yet young....No one of any generosity would think the worse of him for getting private instruction.

Even though Poe's works were more popular than ever, his life was spiraling downward. A few months after he finally achieved his dream of owning his own magazine by using borrowed funds to take over the *Broadway Journal*, the weekly ran out of money. If that were not bad enough, when Poe was invited to read a new poem in America's literary capital of Boston, he showed up drunk and read his early poem "Al Aaraaf" instead. The audience started walking out until he attempted to salvage the evening by reciting "The Raven."

Back in New York, Thomas Dunn English replied to Poe's depiction of him in *The Literati of New York City* by writing in the *Mirror* that Poe was a drunk, a scoundrel, a fraud, a forger and—worst of all—a bad writer. English also recounted the feud with Elizabeth Ellet, placing the blame on Poe for supposedly lying about having received letters from her. Poe responded by suing the *Mirror* for libel. Poe won the lawsuit but lost the war with the New York literati. It should be no surprise that it was during this period, while living in the Amity Street house, that he composed his greatest tale of revenge, "The Cask of Amontillado," in which a man responds to an insult by sealing the one who has insulted him behind a wall to suffocate. Some literary scholars believe that Poe based the story's arrogant and buffoonish victim on none other than Thomas Dunn English.

In February 1846, Virginia handed Edgar a Valentine's Day poem. In lines that began with each letter of his name, she pleaded with him to take her out of the city to a little country cottage where "Love alone shall guide" them and "heal [her] weakened lungs." Edgar, Virginia, Maria and Catterina soon left Amity Street—and New York City—to find a cottage in the country, far from Ellet, English and the rest of the literati.

Visiting Poe's Last Manhattan Residence

In 2001, New York University announced that it was going to demolish Poe's last Manhattan home to make way for a new law school. Despite the best efforts of Poe's admirers, historians and the general public, the university demolished this literary and historical landmark. The school did, however, agree to allow the Poe Museum in Richmond to save some of the bricks, some of which have been incorporated into the museum's garden, which, you will recall, has been hardscaped with bricks salvaged from Poe's homes and places of work.

The university also decided to replicate the façade of Poe's home on the side of its new building. You can find it at 85 West Third Street. Although the façade was constructed from modern materials, the builders preserved a section of the original banister inside. This piece of centuries-old wood is the sole surviving witness to everything that went down there between Edgar, Virginia, Frances, Anne Lynch and Elizabeth Ellet, but it's not talking. We may never know the full story.

Just in case you do not wish to enroll at NYU before your Poe pilgrimage just to visit their law school building, members of the public can see the banister fragment during designated hours. Check their website for details.

Chapter 15

EDGAR ALLAN POE COTTAGE, THE BRONX

An hour's ride by train took Poe from New York City's crowds and filth to the perfumed air of Fordham, a tiny village nestled between rolling hills and woods. The apple orchard was abloom with white flowers, and the cherry trees' snowy petals littered the path leading up to the little white frame cottage perched atop of hill as if about to slide off it. A low porch ran the width of the house. An extension leaned against one end.

Approaching the front door, the visitors passed through the perfume of spring flowers and the music of songbirds to be greeted by a thin man dressed in immaculate black. Poe ushered his guests to sit in the parlor on the left. The smells of Maria Clemm fixing a stew wafted in from the kitchen. The muffled sounds of painful coughing emanated from the wall at the other end of the parlor. It was the kind of cough that hurts the ears of anyone who hears it. Virginia was having a bad day.

With its cozy, idyllic setting, the place felt like something out of one of Poe's poems, but it was actually one of Virginia's poems come to life. Just a few months earlier, on Valentine's Day 1846, Virginia gave her husband an acrostic poem that spelled out his name with the first letter of each line. Unlike most of his poems, hers was clearly written for his eyes alone with no intention of ever publishing it.

These agonized lines plead for her husband to take her far from the city to escape "the tattling of many tongues," specifically the rumors continuing to spread from the despised Mrs. Ellet. Elsewhere in those verses, Virginia

Top: Arthur Alexander Stoughton took this photograph of himself standing in front of Edgar Allan Poe's cottage in 1884. It was in this humble home that Poe composed his classic poems "Annabel Lee" and "The Bells" in addition to writing his final book and magnum opus, *Eureka*.

Bottom: In this 1930 photograph of Edgar Allan Poe's cottage parlor, one can see his favorite rocking chair in front a window from which he could observe the rolling hills and cherry trees stretching out into the distance. The distant ringing of the church bell at nearby Fordham College echoed through the landscape. In the cage hanging above the chair, songbirds filled the cottage with their music.

Mary Bronson, a young visitor to Poe's cottage, was so fascinated with the poet, who apologized to her for not having the pet raven she had expected to see, that she asked her father to commission this daguerreotype portrait of Poe. The author's dapper outfit and fashionable mustache and side whiskers give little indication of the desperate poverty that plagued him.

pleads for Edgar to find her a cottage in the country, where the fresh air might "heal my weakened lungs." Yes, she is describing the tuberculosis that is ravaging her body. At the time, one of the many supposed cures for the disease was cold, fresh air, so, moving to a rural setting seemed like her best hope for recovery.

If Poe's "Annabel Lee," that mournful ballad about a man's undying devotion to his lost love, was, as most contend, written about Virginia, then her Valentine poem is Annabel Lee's own side of the story. These are the verses of a quickly fading Annabel Lee to the lover she will leave behind on earth.

Poe's response was to find an old field hand's cottage in the unspoiled countryside outside the city. Built in 1812, the house belonged to John Valentine, who had bought it and the surrounding two acres for $1,000. Valentine rented the place to the Poes for between $60 and $100, depending on which source you consult.

Their furnishings were simple and sparse. According to a visitor, Mary Gove Nichols, who described the cottage for a February 1, 1863 article in London's *Sixpenny Magazine*,

> *The cottage had an air of taste and gentility that must have been lent to it by the presence of its inmates. So neat, so poor, so unfurnished, and yet so charming a dwelling I never saw. The floor of the kitchen was white as wheaten flour. A table, a chair, and a little stove that it contained, seemed to furnish it perfectly. The sitting-room floor was laid with check matting; four chairs, a light stand, and a hanging bookshelf completed its furniture. There were pretty presentation copies of books on the little shelves, and the Brownings had posts of honour on the stand.*

Poe's 1849 tale "Landor's Cottage" is thought to describe the cottage in detail. Most of the sketch details the exterior; the closing paragraphs relate to the interior:

> *Nothing could be more rigorously simple than the furniture of the parlor. On the floor was an ingrain carpet, of excellent texture—a white ground, spotted with small circular green figures. At the windows were curtains of snowy white jaconet muslin: they were tolerably full, and hung decisively, perhaps rather formally, in sharp, parallel plaits to the floor—just to the floor....The more substantial furniture consisted of a round table, a few chairs (including a large rocking-chair,) and a sofa, or rather "settee": its*

material was plain maple painted a creamy white, slightly interstriped with green—the seat of cane.

Of the home's artwork, he continues,

Its expanse was relieved merely by three of Julien's exquisite lithographs à trois crayons, fastened to the wall without frames. One of these drawings was a scene of Oriental luxury, or rather voluptuousness; another was a "carnival piece," spirited beyond compare; the third was a Greek female head—a face so divinely beautiful, and yet of an expression so provokingly indeterminate, never before arrested my attention.

Although these artworks have not been identified, the artist is Bernard-Romain Julien, a French painter and lithographer. The print of a "female head" is probably the one a young visitor named Mary Elizabeth Bronson LeDuc mentioned in an article she wrote for the July 21, 1860 issue of the *Home Journal*. When Poe saw her staring at it, he assured Mary Elizabeth that the subject was definitely "not the Lost Lenore" of his famous poem "The Raven." In fact, Mary Elizabeth found both Poe and his cottage to be very unlike what she had expected to see after having read some of his melancholy poetry. He even felt the need to apologize for not owning a pet raven.

Aside from these mass-produced prints that Poe apparently could not afford to have framed, he still had the watercolor his mother had left him. Fanny Osgood's husband's portrait of Poe might have been there, but it seems to have been with the printer John Sartain by the time of Poe's death. Poe also owned a few other small watercolors and possibly some of his own pencil sketches.

The parlor's main ornaments were vases of geraniums and violets on the mantel, around the windows, in the corners and inside the fireplace. He complemented their scents with a large glass bottle of perfume on the table.

At night, the room's sole light source was an astral lamp set in the center of the table. Resembling a small glass globe set atop a thin brass or bronze column, the solar lamp resembled a glowing star in the night sky. It burned expensive whale oil. The expense was worth it because it produced a brighter and steadier light than candles. In the upstairs room, Poe illuminated his writing desk with two silver-plated candelabra that held three candles each.

Virginia Poe spent her final days in this bed in the Poes' cottage in Fordham. In the absence of a heavy blanket, Poe covered her with his coat, and their beloved tortoiseshell cat Catterina curled up on Virginia's chest to keep her warm. Despite their best efforts, Virginia finally succumbed to tuberculosis in this bed on January 30, 1847, at the age of twenty-four.

When the Poes first moved into the house, the spring weather seemed to improve Virginia's health. Neighbors recalled seeing her sitting on the front porch while Edgar read the newspaper and Maria knitted. While Poe may no longer have been welcome in the literary circle surrounding Anne Lynch, he still maintained plenty of friendships with other New York writers, even attendees of Lynch's soirees. Among his regular visitors were the author and women's health advocate Mary Gove Nichols and her fourteen-year-old daughter Elma Mary Gove, both of whom later wrote about their experiences.

In her aforementioned account from the *Sixpenny Magazine*, Nichols recalled that Virginia "looked very young; she had large black eyes, and a pearly whiteness of complexion, which was a perfect pallor. Her pale face, her brilliant eyes, and her raven hair gave her an unearthly look. One felt that she was almost a disrobed spirit, and when she coughed it was made certain that she was rapidly passing away."

By fall, Virginia's health was in decline, and Nichols remembered:

> *The autumn came, and Mrs. Poe sank rapidly in consumption, and I saw her in her bed-chamber. Everything here was so neat, so purely clean, so scant and poverty-stricken, that I saw the sufferer with such a heartache as the poor feel for the poor. There was no clothing on the bed, which was only straw, but a snow white spread and sheets. The weather was cold, and the sick lady had the dreadful chills that accompany the hectic fever of consumption. She lay on the straw bed, wrapped in her husband's great-coat, with a large tortoiseshell cat in her bosom. The wonderful cat seemed conscious of her great usefulness. The coat and the cat were the sufferer's only means of warmth, except as her husband held her hands, and her mother her feet.*

In an unpublished manuscript shared with me by its owner, Gove recounted being "taken up to the sick-room to see the beautiful child-wife lying on her white bed and fading away. Great dark eyes, a sweet pale face, and masses of dark hair remain in my memory. Everything white save the eyes and the hair."

Nichols described Maria as "passionately fond of her daughter, and her distress on account of her illness and poverty and misery, was dreadful to see."

One evening, Maria invited Gove to spend the night. On a tour of the house, Maria pointed out Poe's bedroom, stating that it was "Eddy's room."

When Gove wondered at the pile of pillows at the head of the bed so that Edgar would have to sit up while he slept, Maria added, "Eddy cannot sleep if his head lies low."

After dinner, Edgar took Gove out to the front yard to sit in the shade of the trees. Pointing out the scenery around them, Poe said, "Look up over your head at the trees…and see how beautiful is the play of sunlight among the leaves—how the shadow of one leaf falls on another." They remained outside until well after sunset. When the moonlight enveloped her, Poe remarked, "How beautiful you look in the moonlight! You should always sit in the moonlight." Gove found the suggestion laughably impractical.

Both Nichols and Gove told of a picnic in which Poe challenged a group of friends to a leaping contest. Poe's jump far surpassed all others, but on landing, his shoes fell apart. A hush fell over the group because they knew Poe could not afford replacements. Taking her aside, Maria asked Nichols to sell one of Poe's poems to an editor they knew. The proceeds would surely buy a new pair.

Poe's financial hardships had forced him to violate his own ethics by writing positive reviews of mediocre poets for pay. During an afternoon stroll through the woods, Poe confessed to Nichols that he had been "paid a hundred dollars to manufacture opinions for [a poet he despised] and fame for an author." He was likely referring to the New York poet Sarah Anna Lewis, whose husband, Sylvanus Lewis, had paid Poe to flatter his wife's verses in the papers.

"Would you blame a man for not allowing his sick wife to starve?" Poe asked.

Nichols was so concerned with the family's plight that she found a nurse to volunteer to care for Virginia. Marie Louise Shew was an author, women's health advocate and free love practitioner. As a child, she had followed her physician father on house calls, and she continued her medical training at the Jefferson County Institute. When she was sixteen, she married Dr. Joel Shew, a devotee of the "water cure," the emerging field of treating illness by soaking the sufferer in water or pouring water over their head. At twenty-three, she was well-versed enough in the topic to write the well-received book *Water-Cure for Ladies: A Popular Work on the Health, Diet, and Regimen of Females and Children, and the Prevention and Cure of Diseases; with a Full Account of the Processes of Water-Cure*. In addition to advocating soaking in water, she promoted exercise, a balanced diet and abstinence from tobacco and alcohol as the keys to good health. She also took on occasional work as an abortionist.

From her visit to the Poe cottage, she was overwhelmed with sympathy for the family's dire situation. She replaced Virginia's straw mattress with a feather one, provided linens for that bed and treated the sufferer with fresh food and what passed for medicine in those days. One such remedy was Jew's beer, a mixture of beer, honey and tar that appeared to ease Virginia's suffering.

Shew also took an interest in Poe's health. She determined that Poe had an irregular heartbeat and that a lesion on the side of his brain caused him to go insane when he stimulated it by drinking alcohol. Shew herself neither smoked nor drank, and she was a strict vegetarian.

Quickly ingratiating herself into the family, she became every member's trusted confidante (at least according to her own, much later, self-aggrandizing account). She later claimed that Virginia shared with her important letters from Louisa Allan to Poe and that Virginia gave Shew a miniature of him, kissing it before pressing it into Shew's hand.

Shew was able to ease Virginia's pain for at least the last few months of the girl's life. On January 29, 1847, Poe wrote Shew to say, "My poor Virginia still lives, although failing fast and now suffering much pain. May God grant her life until she sees you and thanks you once again! Her bosom is full to overflowing—like my own—with a boundless— inexpressible gratitude to you. Lest she may never see you more—she bids me say that she sends you her sweetest kiss of love and will die blessing you."

Virginia died the following day. In the absence of a burial shroud, Shew wrapped her in the new bed linens. In the first few hours after death, as Virginia's corpse was stiffening with

Shortly after Virginia's death, an artist captured this last image of Poe's beloved wife. The curve of her neck indicates that she was still lying in bed with her sheets wrapped around her in a makeshift shroud. Not wishing her to be remembered in such a condition—with signs of rigor mortis apparent—the Poe family did not permit the picture to be published until forty-six years later.

rigor mortis, Shew sketched her portrait in watercolor on paper. It is obvious that her head is seen from above while slumped over a pillow. The Poe family, who inherited the sketch from Maria Clemm, found it so unpleasant that they refused to allow its reproduction for nearly five decades. Today this is considered the only fully authenticated portrait of Virginia Poe.

Postmortem portraits were common in Poe's time, but their popularity soon exploded with the introduction of photography. In many cases, the only image a family possessed of a lost loved one was one that showed them after death. Some posed their subjects propped up in a chair while others depicted them on a bed or in a casket. An alternative was the plaster death mask created by making a mold of the deceased's face to produce a life-sized plaster replica.

In accordance with the customs of the time, the family covered all the mirrors in the house to prevent Virginia's spirit from seeing her reflection. The body was placed on a parlor table where it could be watched over by her family.

The ritual of grieving also extended to fashion. Both Maria and Edgar dressed in black. Flashy jewelry was forbidden. In its place, they could wear mourning jewelry made of jet or human hair. The length of time one would dress entirely in black depended on the situation. A widow could dress in mourning for years after her husband's death. In fact, Maria Clemm had worn mourning clothes and a widow's cap ever since her husband's death in 1828, and she never stopped dressing like a widow. A husband might only need dress in mourning for six months after his wife's death. A photograph taken of him later that summer shows Poe dressed in a white or cream-colored vest, indicating he was no longer dressed in mourning. He did, however, wear his and Virginia's wedding rings fused together.

Even one's stationery should reflect their grief. Paper with thick black borders served this purpose. One of Poe's calling cards with such a border survives at the University of Texas at Austin.

Another element of mourning was clipping locks of the deceased's hair to give to friends and family members. One such lock of Virginia's hair is now owned by the Poe Society of Baltimore and resides in the Enoch Pratt Free Library. In the absence of more of her poems or more than a fragment of one of her letters, these few strands are about the best source of information on her daily life in her final years. At almost fifteen inches long, the hair contains the heavy metals present in her environment over the course of roughly two years.

In 2002, the Poe Society allowed Alliance Atlantic to test a few of the strands for a documentary to air on Discovery Health Channel. In a study designed by Albert Donnay and conducted by Drs. John Ejnik and Jose Centeno at the Department of Environmental and Toxicologic Pathology, U.S. Armed Forces Institute of Pathology in Washington, D.C., they analyzed the levels of heavy metals present in the samples. The scientists cut Virginia's hair in half in order to test the two ends separately. The end closest to her scalp had grown during her time in the Fordham cottage, and the other end grew during her residence in New York City. Then they tested the two ends separately and compared them with a sample of Poe's hair taken after his death. His sample grew during the years he lived in the countryside, while hers recorded the chemicals present in her environment when she was living in New York City. These results were compared with those of Edgar's hair, which grew entirely during his time in Fordham.

The results showed that she was right to move to the country. When she was in the city, her arsenic levels were forty-five times today's normal levels and twice the level at which symptoms of arsenic poisoning become evident. The arsenic could have been present in her drinking water or in the coal oil they burned for lighting. Her levels dropped by 66 percent when she was living in the country. Edgar's levels were consistent with the second reading, indicating they had similar exposure.

Her nickel and uranium levels also dropped when she moved to Fordham. Her lead and mercury levels, which were both high in New York, stayed high in Fordham. Since Edgar's levels differed from hers, her lead and mercury likely came not from her environment but from mercury-based medicines or lead white makeup. Of course, it would be well over a century and a half before scientists were able to conduct these kinds of tests and it would be almost as long before the public realized the dangers of heavy metal exposure.

Since the Poes could not afford to bury Virginia, Shew and Poe's old Baltimore friend Mary Starr stepped forward to provide a coffin, a shroud and mourning clothes for Edgar. The funeral took place on a day so cold that Starr stayed in the cottage rather than join the mourners at graveside. Eliza White had come from Richmond to join them. Virginia's and Edgar's cousin Elizabeth Rebecca Herring joined them from Baltimore. The rest of the attendees were friends, writers and editors from New York.

For eleven years, she had been Poe's greatest supporter, always convinced of his talent and never losing faith that one day he would achieve the fame and fortune for which he had striven ever since he ran away from John

Allan's home two decades earlier. Without her, Poe was lost. He had lost his reason for living. His health was failing, and the newspapers reported that he was not long for the grave.

Looking over his manuscript for "Eulalie," his poem celebrating the joys of married life, he took out his pencil and wrote on the back,

Deep in earth my love is lying
And I must weep alone.

Two weeks later, on Valentine's Day, he composed a poem in honor of Marie Louise Shew, whose selfless service had comforted all of them over the previous months. When he published "To M.L.S." in the *Home Journal*, the editor prefaced it, "The following seems said over a hand clasped in the speaker's two. It is by Edgar A. Poe, and is evidently the pouring out of a very deep feeling of gratitude."

Shew continued to care for the Poes and became their trusted friend. She even helped him compose one of his most celebrated poems. That spring, Poe was answering a challenge to write something unlike anything he had ever done before. Until then, Poe adhered to a philosophy, which he spelled out in the essay "The Philosophy of Composition," that a successful poem should leave a single impression on the reader. If a poem were to be melancholy, then every word and every line should contribute to that feeling. He went so far as to claim that he began his poems at the end, with the final line he intended to leave an impression on his ideal reader, and then he would write the rest of the poem leading up to that ending.

Now, Poe wanted to see if he could write a poem that explored

According to Poe's nurse Marie Louise Shew, this Sheffield silver candelabrum was lighting the poet's desk when he wrote "The Bells." This artifact came to the Poe Museum in Richmond from Shew's youngest sister, Elva P. Barney.

a wide range of emotions without losing its sense of unity. And he would have written it if only the bells at St. John's would stop ringing long enough for him to concentrate. When he would not stop complaining to Shew about the racket, she took his pen and wrote, "The Bells" at the top of his page. Then she jotted down the first line. He answered by scribbling the second. She composed another verse, and he ended up finishing the poem "The Bells."

Poe seems to have corroborated that story by writing beneath the title of the manuscript for the poem now owned by the University of Texas at Austin, "By Mrs. M.L. Shew." Nearby Fordham University claims to have the actual bell that inspired the poem. Long since retired from service, the large iron bell has since come to be known as Old Edgar Allan, and a bronze plaque claims that it "is said to have inspired Poe, a friend and neighbor, to write his celebrated poem, 'The Bells.'" Shew, however, claimed it was a different bell from a different church.

Shew might also have inspired another poem. When she told Poe about the lesion she believed he had on the side of his brain, she also informed him that his heart beat no more than ten times before it intermitted. In response, Poe wrote the verses,

The pulse beats ten and intermits;
God nerve the soul that ne'er forgets
In calm or storm, by night or day,
Its steady toil, its loyalty.

He titled the poem, which he dedicated to Shew, "The Beloved Physician." No one knows more of the poem than a handful of dimly remembered verses because, after Shew heard that Poe had sold the poem to a magazine, she paid him more to sell it to her instead. Then she destroyed it to prevent anyone else from ever reading it. She thought it was too personal, too revealing. She was, after all, a married woman. She explained that her husband had more old-fashioned views of marriage than she did.

Besides composing poetry in the cottage, Poe also began work on his magnum opus, his great "theory of everything." What began as a lecture called "The Universe" evolved into a book-length philosophical and cosmological essay titled *Eureka*. To call it an essay is misleading because it transcends genres. Beginning with a humorous short story, the work transitions into page after page of Poe's ideas about matter, energy, space, time, how everything began and how it will end. If that sounds like a lot to cover in one essay, Poe realizes this, stating in the opening paragraphs that, "I design to speak of the Physical, Metaphysical and Mathematical—of the Material and Spiritual Universe: —of its Essence, its Origin, its Creation, its Present Condition and its Destiny."

He insists that he will challenge the theories proposed by history's greatest thinkers with a new idea that connects everything to a single particle so dense that it would cease to exist. *Eureka* presents an early version of the Big Bang theory and describes chaos theory, black holes and multiple universes. This is mixed with a current of mysticism, talk of past lives in other universes and the reality of dreams. Somehow, it all fits together because, in Poe's view, the universe is a poem. To Poe, who believes that constructing a rhymed poem is the greatest challenge for a genius, God must be a poet.

God was also present in all matter. As Poe explained three years earlier in a letter to James Russell Lowell,

> *I have no belief in spirituality. I think the word a mere word. No one has really a conception of spirit. We cannot imagine what is not.... The unparticlet matter, permeating & impelling, all things, is God. Its activity is the thought of God—which creates. Man, and other thinking beings, are individualizations of the unparticled matter. Man exists as a "person," by being clothed with matter (the particled matter) which individualizes him.*

Meanwhile, Shew was trying to reintroduce Poe to Christianity. On the following Christmas Eve, she took Poe to a church service with her in Manhattan. He stood, holding one side of her hymnal as he sang in a beautiful tenor. Everything was going well until the minister started repeating the phrase "He was a man of sorrows and acquainted with grief." At that, Poe rushed out of the building and waited outside for Shew to join him after the sermon. She was beginning to have her doubts about the state of Poe's soul, but she was not ready to give up on him yet.

The next Valentine's Day, he wrote her another poem. This time, he exercised greater discretion by titling it "To — — ." The poem, as originally published, is far from one of his best, but the manuscript version he delivered to her, to be seen by no one else, reveals much more of his passion than is normally found in his public works. In the six lines removed from the poem's final draft, he calls Marie Louise by name and writes of "the palpitating tide of passion" flowing over him. If Poe had tried to publish those lines, she might have felt compelled to burn that one, too.

When *Eureka* finally went to press, his publisher agreed to print a small run of 500 copies—49,500 fewer copies than Poe expected—and he received an advance of only fourteen dollars, which is less than he was paid for "The Raven." Over the past year, he had earned less from his writing than he did for suing the *New York Mirror*.

Shew's spiritual adviser John Henry Hopkins read the book and was horrified. He thought Poe must be an unredeemable atheist or deist or pantheist. Whatever he was, Poe was bad for Shew's spiritual well-being. Hopkins advised her to cut off all contact with him immediately, so she did.

Naturally, this betrayal devastated Poe, but it did not take long to recover. Interested women had already started showing up on his doorstep within months of Virginia's death. Sarah Anna Lewis was making such frequent (and annoying) appearances that he started running out the back door and hiding in the woods as soon as he saw her approach the cottage.

From Richmond, his friend Eliza White came to visit him and looked through some of his old sketches of Elmira. From Lowell, Massachusetts, Jane Ermina Locke started writing him in 1847, but a year later, he still had not met her. Since she dodged questions about her age and marital status in her letters, he naturally assumed that she was a young widow. It wasn't until she paid a visit to the cottage that he discovered she was middle-aged and married. That did not prevent her from inviting him to stay with her (and her husband) in Lowell. Once he got there, he was distracted by her younger cousin Nancy Richmond and moved into her house for the rest of his stay. Of course, she was also married.

Nancy, whom Poe nicknamed Annie, was the subject of his poem "For Annie," which was also written in the Fordham cottage. She visited Poe at home and charmed both him and Maria. If not for her refusal to leave her husband, she would have been the perfect woman for him. But, because she was off-limits, she encouraged him to devote himself to someone else.

By the summer of 1848, he heard from the Mackenzies in Richmond that Elmira Shelton was a widow and that she might be amenable to a visit, so he traveled down to Richmond. Then he got news that pulled him back north.

In Providence, Rhode Island, the poet Sarah Helen Whitman had taken an interest in Poe. Already a respected writer, well-known in the Boston and New York literary scenes, Whitman was friendly with leading writers and editors like Sarah Josepha Hale, Ralph Waldo Emerson, Frances Osgood and Anne Charlotte Lynch. Whitman was intelligent, eccentric and interested in all the latest mystical ideas, including Spiritualism. She was also an abolitionist and a supporter of women's rights. If that were not enough, she was an independent personality known for dressing all in white and wearing a coffin-shaped pendant. When she was not writing, she cared for her elderly mother and her mentally ill sister and tended to her backyard rose garden.

Long before she met Poe, she was fascinated by his works and started asking her New York friends about him. Unbeknownst to her, Poe had once spied on her from a distance. It was in 1845, during a trip to Providence with Frances Osgood. It was such a hot night that he found it impossible to sleep and decided to wander the empty city. Walking up a hill, he saw a woman dressed in white, sitting among her rose garden in the moonlight. Having heard descriptions of her, Poe knew exactly who she was, but he did not approach her. He did not speak or attract her attention. He just stood in the shadows and watched her.

Three years later, on the same Valentine's Day that Poe wrote his second Valentine poem for Marie Louise Shew, Whitman sent her own composition to be read at Anne Lynch's annual Valentine's Day soiree. Lynch was horrified to see the title: "To Edgar A. Poe."

In its ten stanzas, Whitman portrays herself as a dove who wants to fly away with the Raven to his "lofty eyrie." The message could not be clearer.

When all the guests at Lynch's party read their Valentines aloud, Lynch recited Whitman's, reporting back to the author,

> *Our party last Monday evening every one said was very brilliant.—There was an immense crowd, many more than I expected....Your valentines were all read some of them I have sent to the Home Journal at the request of Morris & Willis....The one to Poe I admired exceedingly & would like to have published with your consent with the others, but he is in such bad odour with most persons who visit me that if I were to receive him, I should lose the company of many whom I value more. [Name redacted] will not go where he visits & several others have an inveterate prejudice against him.*

Whitman's poem was not among those Lynch sent to the *Home Journal* for publication, explaining to the poet, "I really do not think it would be any advantage to you to publish the Valentine to Poe not because it is not beautiful in itself but there is a deeply rooted prejudice against him which I trust he will overcome."

Rather than publishing the manuscript, Lynch handed it to Frances Osgood to convey it to Poe. When Poe finally saw it, he ripped his old poem

"To Helen" out of a book and mailed it, without a cover letter, to Whitman. Just how Poe expected her to respond to this is unknown, but he soon sent her a new poem in which he describes the night he watched her in her rose garden. This time, she recognized his handwriting from the previous poem's envelope and responded by publishing another poem in the *Home Journal*. This one referenced passages from Poe's recent poem to her.

Poe could not wait any longer. He cut short his Richmond trip and headed back to Fordham. Using an assumed name, he wrote her a letter pretending to request her autograph. He was really just trying to find out if she was home so he could visit her. He went to Providence anyway.

Poe and Whitman took a long, romantic walk through the Swan Point Cemetery, and he was hooked. He pleaded with her to marry him, but her mother objected to the match, suspecting Poe was a gold-digger.

When Poe got back to Fordham, he carried on a correspondence with Whitman. This did not stop him from writing to Annie—or from taking a trip with Annie to her family's farm, where he held her hand by the fire. But the still-married Annie persuaded Poe to continue his pursuit of the single Whitman.

When Poe refocused his attention on Whitman, her mother insisted that he sign a prenuptial agreement to make sure the family's money was off-limits to the penniless poet. Poe also swore to her that rumors of his drunkenness were greatly exaggerated, but he ultimately resorted to desperate measures to convince her to marry him. One night, after leaving her, he proceeded to Boston, where he acquired a vial of laudanum, a solution of opium in alcohol and wrote a letter to Annie Richmond, pleading with her to join him at his bedside for his death.

Swallowing half of the drug, he stumbled to the post office to mail the letter—only to collapse on the way. He was fortunate to be recognized and picked up by some of Whitman's friends, who cared for him until he recovered well enough to leave under his own power.

In need of some quick cash, he sat for a daguerreotypist who apparently paid Poe for the sitting in order to sell copies of the resultant photo. The worst picture ever taken of Poe, it depicts a haggard, broken man, barely holding himself together while remaining defiant. He stares straight at the camera with a sneer on his lips. Today, that photo is the best-known image of Poe, the one in a million internet memes. Back then, it was a document of the low point in Poe's life.

A week later, Poe and Whitman were engaged on the condition that he abstain from alcohol. The engagement lasted one month. She broke up with him two days before Christmas—and one day before their wedding announcement hit the papers.

Back in Fordham, Maria was overjoyed that the wedding had been called off. She wrote to Annie to inform her that the newspapers were wrong—that the wedding had been canceled. Poe wrote one last letter to Whitman, letting her know that he would never speak ill of her, even to defend himself. Now he was free to pursue Annie.

Poe was back at the writing desk, generating new content for the *Dollar Newspaper* and *Godey's Lady's Book*, among other periodicals. He commenced, and later abandoned, another book project, *Literary America*, which would have featured a series of his profiles of famous

This is both the best and the worst photograph of Poe. The daguerreotype was taken by Edwin Manchester in Providence, Rhode Island, on November 9, 1848, four days after Poe's failed suicide attempt and four days before he became engaged to the poet Sarah Helen Whitman.

authors. Cutting apart the manuscript, he sold the essay about Frances Osgood to the *Southern Literary Messenger*, which started buying his essays and reviews on a regular basis. When not composing new articles, poems or short stories, he was penciling corrections into his copy of *Eureka* in preparation for a revised edition.

Poe was by then so famous that he became the subject of parody and satire. Both James Russell Lowell and Augustine J.H. Duganne ridiculed him in verse, and Thomas Dunn English, his old enemy from their time in New York, mocked Poe in prose. English hardly let an issue of his new magazine *The John-Donkey* pass without insulting Poe on its pages. Several authors had already published parodies of "The Raven," but English went even further by composing humorous poems in the manner of Poe. One of them, "The Lady Hubbard," retells the nursery rhyme "Old Mother Hubbard" as if Poe had written it.

The first half of 1849 was a productive time for Poe. While he was in the cottage, he wrote several of his great late works, including the antislavery fable "Hop-Frog" and the poems "Eldorado," "For Annie" and "A Dream

This is the earliest known copy of the last daguerreotype taken of Poe before his death in 1849. It shows him in Richmond, about two weeks before his demise in Baltimore. Since the original has been damaged and has been missing for over a century, this 1855 tintype is the best record of its appearance. Literary collector Susan Jaffe Tane donated the tintype to the Poe Museum in 2020.

Within a Dream." He also finally completed the third and final version of "The Bells." He could not have done it without his beloved mother-in-law Maria Clemm, who acted as his business manager, cook and mother; so, in that last year of his life, Poe dedicated his new poem "To My Mother" to her.

For the first time since Virginia's death, he was beginning to feel optimistic about the future. Off and on for nearly a decade, he had pursued the dream of starting his own literary magazine, and after all that time, it finally seemed attainable. He printed a prospectus for his proposed *Stylus* and sent copies to possible financial backers. In a November 28, 1848 letter to Frances Allan's cousin Edward Valentine, Poe wrote on a copy of the prospectus, "After a long and bitter struggle with illness, poverty, and the thousand evils which attend them, I find myself, at length, in a position to establish myself permanently and to triumph over all difficulties." That is, if Valentine could but loan him $200. Valentine was unable to contribute to Poe's dream project, but a young editor in Illinois stepped forward with some of the funds. Poe just needed to round up subscribers and a few more backers by taking a lecture tour on friendly soil. Since Poe had already lectured throughout the North, he planned a series of appearances in southern cities in which he had not yet performed.

Ever since his editorship of the *Southern Literary Messenger*, he had been popular with southern readers—even if his years in the North and association with abolitionists like James Russell Lowell had prejudiced a few of them against him.

That summer, after another visit to Annie in Lowell, Poe left the cottage for the last time. He was heading south for Richmond.

Poe died in Baltimore on his way back to New York. Maria Clemm did not learn of his death until after his funeral. Annie wrote to her, telling Maria to sell off everything she didn't need and to stay with the Richmonds in Lowell. After disposing of Poe's rocking chair, Virginia's bed, her soup ladle and most of the rest of her possessions, Maria packed a trunk of a few cherished mementos of Edgar and Virginia and moved in with Annie. As for Catterina, Maria discovered that the beloved family cat had died the same day Poe did.

THE POE COTTAGE AFTER POE

As soon as word of Poe's death reached her, Annie wrote to Muddy, "Sell off everything, and so forth." Poe's mother-in-law gathered up her most valuable possessions and sold the rest.

Before the ink was dry on his hatchet job of an obituary, Griswold came calling for Poe's manuscripts. He managed to convince Muddy that he, the esteemed editor of *The Poets and Poetry of America*, was ideally suited to edit the first posthumous edition of Poe's works, so she appointed him Poe's literary executor. Unable to pay for Griswold's services, she signed over the rights to Poe's works to him. Never mind that, as Poe's closest living relative, Rosalie should have inherited the rights, so Muddy had no legal authority to sell them to anyone. It gets worse. Both she and Rosalie retained lawyers. With Griswold acting on her behalf, Muddy engaged in a battle with Poe's sister over who got to keep Poe's empty trunk (the manuscripts it once held having already gone to Griswold). When all the dust had settled, Rosalie got the trunk, Griswold issued the first complete collection of Poe's works with his malicious biography of Poe and Muddy got some free copies of the book.

Poe's mother-in-law Maria Clemm used this brass soup ladle while living in their cottage near Fordham, New York. After Poe's death, Annie Richmond advised her to sell everything and move in with her friends. This is one of the items she sold, and the daughter of the buyer donated it to the Poe Museum.

The cottage did not sit empty for long. With all the artists making sketches, engravings and paintings of it, the new owners undoubtedly knew of the place's famous former occupant. Some of the tenants even found the time to guide Poe pilgrims on tours of the house, pointing out where Poe slept or where he composed his poetry.

When she visited a quarter century after Poe's death, Martha J. Lamb, who described the event for the July 18, 1874 issue of *Appleton's Journal*, encountered a very helpful but misinformed host who identified for her Poe's bedroom, his cow-house and the room in which she said Maria Clemm used to lock him up for days at a time.

By then, the old walls were already giving way to the onslaught of the elements and the weight of an encroaching tangle of vines. Just as nature was reclaiming the dry boards and slates, civilization was storming the gates. The city was growing, bisecting the property with new roads as new buildings sprouted out of freshly cleared land. The little cemetery that held Virginia Poe's remains was standing in the way of progress and needed to go. Who would stand up to save her bones—and Poe's crumbling cottage?

It was at this point that William Fearing Gill entered the picture. One of the most colorful characters in the Poe community, Gill was a thin man with an oversized mustache covering half his face. With what must have been boundless energy, Gill juggled acting, editing, writing and investing in get-rich-quick schemes. Above all this, he considered his true calling to be the defense of Poe's good name from the attacks of Griswold and his disciples. For years, Poe's admirers had written articles calling out Griswold's lies and distortions, and Poe's former fiancée Sarah Helen Whitman went so far as to publish a book titled *Edgar Poe and His Critics* with the expressed purpose of putting to rest Griswold's "sick and deplorable attacks" on the defenseless dead poet. It was over two decades after Poe's death that his first British biographer sought to research and write the definitive Poe biography by interviewing those who had known the poet best. John Henry Ingram corresponded with Sarah Helen Whitman, Annie Richmond, Marie Louise Shew, Stella Lewis and other Poe associates who could (in theory, at least) provide him a long-awaited factual account of Poe's life. Sure, Whitman, Richmond, Shew and Lewis were slightly less interested in facts than they were in letting the world know the central position they all thought they held in Poe's life. Two of them even claimed to have been the inspiration for "Annabel Lee." But they were the best Ingram had, and his would be the most accurate Poe biography to date, with the possible exception of Gill's.

About this time, Gill started writing his own biography, using many of the same sources. The timing seemed a little bit more than coincidental to Gill, who accused Ingram in print of plagiarism. Ingram fired back that he had never even heard of Gill or his project.

Gill's Poe book sold well enough to go through multiple editions within the first few years. With each new edition, he added more information to the book's appendix, and it was in the appendix of the fifth edition, printed in 1880, that he added an account of his visit to Virginia Poe's grave, related how he had personally rescued her remains from the gravedigger to save them from being thrown into a mass grave to make way for new construction.

As with most of Gill's stories, there may or may not be any truth to it. He likely took something from the cemetery that day, but we cannot be certain what it was. At least, he told everyone it was Virginia Poe's bones that reposed in the small box under his bed for the next seven years.

Given the guests who reported how disturbing the sight of these bones was, none of them were able to convince him to give them up. According to Gill, it was Poe's ghost who finally contacted him through the form of a raven that flew in through his window.

Virginia's bones (or whoever's remains they were) were finally transferred to Baltimore to be buried next to her husband in 1885, but Gill's Poe fixation was far from over.

Gill eventually married Edith Olive Gwynne, the sister-in-law of millionaire Cornelius Vanderbilt. During their brief but turbulent union, Gill and his new bride wined and dined in Paris and spent the family money as quickly as it poured in. Even after the two divorced, Gill retained a house and an allowance from the Vanderbilts. It must have been their money that allowed him to purchase the Poe cottage at auction for the rock-bottom price of $750 in 1895.

By this time, the crumbling structure was in desperate need of repair. To make matters worse, newer, bigger buildings were crowding out the tiny cottage. The porch that once overlooked a grove of cherry trees now faced the wall of an adjacent building. It looked like Poe's last home was about to be leveled to make way for progress, but there was one last hope. It was a controversial idea. Maybe the house could be moved across the street. Some argued that picking up and moving the cottage from its original spot would deprive it of much of its historical context. Others thought that creating a park to simulate its original setting would be more historically accurate than leaving it wedged between two modern structures. Either way, Gill was not up to the task.

Poe Cottage Monument & Park, New York

In this photo taken in Poe Park in the Bronx in 1909, one struggles to see the tiny cottage once occupied by Poe, as it is nearly hidden to the right of the large apartment building on the left side of the image. Four years later, the cottage would be moved to save it from destruction.

The New York Shakespeare Society took over the house as its headquarters and intended to restore it to the way it appeared during the period of Poe's residence. The Society generated enough interest that luminaries from Theodore Roosevelt to Rudyard Kipling lent their support by urging the New York state legislature to fund the project. It took a decade, but in 1905, the legislature finally contributed $100,000 to create a park across the street where the house could be moved before it was too late.

It was a busy time for Poe promotion. Poe organizations across the country were preparing for the Poe centennial in 1909, and the Bronx was no different. On Poe's one hundredth birthday, January 19, 1909, the Bronx Society of Arts and Sciences hosted a day of festivities featuring readings of Poe's poems, speeches, music and a recitation of "The Raven" accompanied by an orchestra. The climax of the day's events was the unveiling of a new bronze bust of the poet in Poe Park. It did not take long for neighborhood kids to vandalize the sculpture, which had to be moved inside the cottage for protection.

Four years later, the city moved the cottage across the street to its new home 150 yards away in Poe Park. While the location does not replicate its previous setting atop a low hill, the new spot gives the house more breathing room and a grassy front yard. And that is where the house remains.

Since it was built around 1812 and stayed there until 1913, that means the house has been in its current location longer than it was on its original site, and more people from around the globe have seen Poe's cottage in Poe Park than ever visited it when it was across the street.

Among the countless people who visited were two neighborhood kids, Bob Kane and Bill Finger, who were sitting on a bench in Poe Park in 1939, reflecting on the success of the Superman comics. They decided to come up with their own superhero—a darker, more mysterious, more Poe-esque sort of hero who lurks the city at night. He would be a master detective, a nod to Poe's fictional detective Dupin. It would be just the sort of superhero Poe might have created. That is how, in the shadow of Poe's cottage (maybe with a little help from Poe's spirit), Kane and Finger created Batman. Considering how Poe helped shaped the development of Batman, it should be no surprise that Poe and Batman joined forces in 2003 for the comic series *Batman Nevermore*.

In 1965, the Belgian Surrealist painter Rene Magritte made his first visit to the United States to attend the opening of an exhibit of his works in New York's Museum of Modern Art. When asked what he would like to see during his stay, he said, the "Poe Shrine." The notoriously deadpan Magritte wept while walking through the Poe Cottage. It should not come as a shock that the painter of raining bowler-hatted men was a Poe fan. Throughout his pictures, Magritte used Poe titles or placed Poe references, including a copy of Poe's book *The Narrative of Arthur Gordon Pym* in the painting *Reproduction Prohibited*. Even when the Poe references are not so obvious, the influence is there. When explaining his painting of a bird's egg in a bird cage, Magritte quoted a passage from *Eureka* (which Poe wrote in the cottage) as the central idea behind the image.

The cottage's visitors might not all be among the living. At least one paranormal investigator believed that Poe's ghost might linger in his former home. In 1980, Stephen Kaplan of the Parapsychology Institute of America was examining the house when he took a photograph of Poe's rocking chair. When he developed the picture, Kaplan saw a white blur in the middle. He set aside the photo. The next time Kaplan glanced at the picture, the blur had become a bit more distinct—more human. Over the course of several weeks, what once was a nebulous smudge became the translucent shape of a man sitting in Poe's rocking chair. Eventually,

In 1913, the Poe cottage was moved from its original location to its current spot, as seen in this photo taken by the author a century later in Poe Park. It is now operated by the Bronx County Historical Society and is open to the public.

the man's features grew to resemble those of none other than the chair's former owner. In his book *True Tales of the Unknown*, Kaplan concluded, "Poe's spirit remains with the living; he is eternally rocking in a rocking chair, not only in a cottage in the Bronx, New York, but also in a carefully guarded photograph."

VISITING THE POE COTTAGE

Poe pilgrims can see the Poe Cottage in Poe Park at Kingsbridge Road and the Grand Concourse. The easiest way to get there from Manhattan is by subway. Take either the D or 4 train to the Kingsbridge Road stop. From there, it is a short walk to the cottage. Be sure to call ahead or check their website to make sure the cottage will be open and to find out what special exhibits will be on display in the Poe Park visitors center, which is, incidentally, shaped like a raven (when seen from the right angle). Make sure you have enough time for a tour of the site. It may be small, but there are some Poe treasures you will not want to miss. Look out for the bed in which Virginia Poe died, Poe's favorite rocking chair and Edmond T. Quinn's bronze bust of Poe. Over the course of your Poe pilgrimage, you might have seen plaster copies at the Baltimore Poe House, the Providence Athenaeum, the Library of Virginia and the Poe Museum; this one is the original.

I visited the cottage at the invitation of its former director of programs and external relations Angel Hernandez, who gave me a private tour. He led me from the foyer to a tiny room nearly filled with Virginia's bed. This is where Poe would have lingered by her side for hours, watching over her with Catterina asleep on her chest. Angel opened the half-door to let me step inside the room in which Virginia breathed her last. The very bed in which she died back on January 30, 1847, is one of the few Poe family possessions to remain in the house, and it is surely the most powerful. Some say it was tubercular meningitis or delirium tremens that caused Poe's death two years later, but it was Virginia's death—right here in this room—that really killed him.

At the other end of the first floor was the kitchen where Maria Clemm prepared meals for the family and their many guests.

Then we ascended a narrow back staircase to see the second-floor bedrooms, the larger of which was Poe's. He might have used the smaller room for writing, but, because it had no fireplace, he probably used the parlor during the winter months. Those rooms now showcase artwork and an orientation video, but behind the modern touches, one can still get a sense of Poe's presence in those rooms.

My favorite room would have to be the parlor, and not just because Angel let me cross the stanchions to get a closer look at Poe's rocking chair. No, Poe wasn't sitting there that day. This is the place where Poe entertained his guests—including Rosalie Poe, Annie Richmond, Marie Louise Shew, Mary Gove Nichols and more. These walls once vibrated with his stirring recitations of "The Raven." This is also where he kept his desk, so it must have been where he wrote "Annabel Lee," "The Bells" and, of course, *Eureka*. The view outside the window may have changed since then, but the atmosphere inside that parlor is still pure Poe.

The Poe family's possessions from their time in Fordham have spread far and wide since 1849. The Poe Museum in Richmond owns Maria Clemm's soup ladle and Virginia's mirror. Virginia Poe's miniature drinking glass and perfume bottle are in the collection of the Poe Society of Baltimore and are housed in the Enoch Pratt Free Library. Some of Poe's books, including his copy of Aesop's *Fables*, reside in the Harry Ransom Center at the University of Texas at Austin. The Poe family Bible, given to Poe by Maria Clemm, is unlocated but is probably in the New York Public Library. Poe's copy of *Eureka*, with his corrections penciled onto several pages and a paragraph added to the end, survives in a private collection. The manuscripts on which Poe worked while living there are in too many public and private collections to mention. As an example, there are at least four manuscript copies of "Annabel Lee." These can be found in Columbia University, the Philadelphia Free Library, the Morgan Pierpont Library and Harvard University. Poe's West Point greatcoat, the one he wore for two of his six photographs and which he used to cover Virginia during her final illness, is lost. Angel told me an elderly Bronxite recalled it had been discarded in the 1930s because "it was old."

CONCLUSION

*P*oe died in transit. He was passing through Baltimore to catch a train on his way from Richmond, where he had spent the summer, and Philadelphia, where he had lined up an editing assignment to complete before traveling north to New York to see Maria Clemm. He left his luggage in Richmond's Swan Tavern, which had confiscated it due to lack of payment. He forgot his boot hooks at his sister's home, Duncan Lodge, where he stayed after being thrown out of the Swan Tavern and finding other options too expensive. Other possessions were scattered in the Bronx, Baltimore and various homes he had visited. Many of these possessions can be seen today at the Poe Museum in Richmond, the only Poe museum that is not also a Poe home. Like these relics, his life had been scattered between various sites and cities. He was restless, always in search of the next opportunity to realize his literary ambitions.

As the preceding chapters should have made evident, Poe's life was never easy. He may not have lived long enough to realize all of his dreams, but he died without regrets. Ten months before he drew his final breath, he wrote to his friend F.W. Thomas on February 14, 1849,

> *Literature is the most noble of professions. In fact, it is about the only one fit for a man. For my own part, there is no seducing me from the path. I shall be a litterateur, at least, all my life; nor would I abandon the hopes which still lead me on for all the gold in California. Talking of gold, and*

Top: At the time of his death in 1849, Poe kept most of his worldly possessions in this black leather trunk. At one point, it contained notes, manuscripts, books, clothing and toiletries. His sister, Rosalie, obtained it and left it to her foster niece, from whom it came to the Poe Museum in 1922. This photograph was taken in the museum's garden pergola shortly after the trunk's arrival.

Bottom: Journalist Tula Pendleton Cumming was researching a 1905 article about Poe when she gained entry into the condemned Swan Tavern and took this, the only known interior photograph of the building in which Poe stayed during his last visit to Richmond. His trunk of clothes was found there after his death. The tavern's owner had confiscated the poet's luggage when the latter failed to pay his bill.

of the temptations at present held out to "poor-devil authors," did it ever strike you that all which is really valuable to a man of letters—to a poet in especial—is absolutely unpurchaseable? Love, fame, the dominion of intellect, the consciousness of power, the thrilling sense of beauty, the free air of Heaven, exercise of body & mind, with the physical and moral health which result—these and such as these are really all that a poet cares for.

As you embark on your Poe pilgrimage, I hope you, like Poe, find what you are searching for.

Appendix

WHERE POE LIVED

BOSTON (62 Carver Street)
January 1809 (born)–May 1809

NEW YORK
May 1809–July 1810

RICHMOND
August 1810–January 1811

CHARLESTON
January 1811–June 1811

NORFOLK
June 1811–August 1811

RICHMOND
August 1811–December 1811 (Boardinghouse near Ninth and Grace Streets)
December 1811–June 1815 (Allan House at Thirteenth and Main Streets)

IRVINE, SCOTLAND (Bridgegate House)
August 1815

LONDON (No. 47 Southampton Row, Russell Square)
October 1815–April 1816

CHELSEA, London, England (Miss Dubourg's boarding school at 146
    Sloane Street)
April 1816 – July 1817

STOKE NEWINGTON, England (Manor House boarding school)
July 1817–June 1820

RICHMOND (Ellis House at Second and Franklin Streets)
August 1820–December 1820

RICHMOND (Allan House at Fifth and Clay Streets)
December 1820–June 1822

RICHMOND (Allan House at Fourteenth and Tobacco Alley)
June 1822–June 1825

RICHMOND (Moldavia at Fifth and Main Streets)
June 1825–February 1826

UNIVERSITY OF VIRGINIA (First on the Lawn and then at 13 or 17 West Range)
February 1826–December 1826

RICHMOND (Moldavia)
December 1826–March 1827

BOSTON
March 1827–May 1827

FORT INDEPENDENCE, Boston Harbor
May 1827–October 1827

FORT MOULTRIE, South Carolina
November 1827–December 1828

FORT MONROE, Virginia
December 1828–April 1829

BALTIMORE (29 Caroline Street)
May 1829–June 1829

BALTIMORE (Beltzhoover's Hotel)
June 1829–June 1830

WEST POINT, New York (28 South Barracks)
June 1830–February 1831

NEW YORK
February 1831–May 1831

BALTIMORE (Mechanics Row, Wilks Street)
May 1831–Early 1833

BALTIMORE (3 Amity Street)
Early 1833–August 1835

RICHMOND (Mrs. Poore's boardinghouse, Ninth and Bank Street)
August 1835–September 1835

RICHMOND (Mrs. Yarrington's boardinghouse, Twelfth and Bank Street)
October 1835–May 1836

RICHMOND (tenement on Seventh Street)
May 1836–February 1837

NEW YORK (Sixth Avenue and Waverley Place)
February 1837–May 1837

NEW YORK (113½ Carmine Street)
May 1837–Early 1838

PHILADELPHIA (202 Mulberry [or Arch] Street)
Early 1838–September 1838

PHILADELPHIA (Sixteenth Street)
September 1838–May 1842

PHILADELPHIA
May 1842–September 1842

PHILADELPHIA (Coates Street)
September 1842–April 1843

PHILADELPHIA (234 [now 530] North Seventh Street)
April 1843–April 1844

NEW YORK (130 Greenwich Street)
April 1844–June 1844

NEW YORK (Brennen Farm, near present-day Broadway and Eighty-Fourth
    Street)
June 1844–January 1845

Poe stayed for part of his last Richmond visit in the Swan Tavern on Broad Street. Once a fashionable establishment frequented by the likes of Thomas Jefferson, it had fallen into disrepair by Poe's time. It still proved too expensive, and he moved to cheaper quarters by the end of the summer.

Duncan Lodge, the house in which Poe's sister, Rosalie Mackenzie Poe, lived with her foster mother, Jane Scott Mackenzie, is the last place Poe spent the night in Richmond before boarding a steamboat for his ill-fated trip to Baltimore. He stayed in the second-floor room directly above the front door.

NEW YORK (154 Greenwich Street or 15 Amity Street)
January 1845–May 1845

NEW YORK (195 East Broadway)
May 1845–October 1845

NEW YORK (85 Amity Street)
October 1845–February 1846

NEW YORK (Turtle Bay, near the present Seventy-Fourth Street)
February 1846–May 1846

NEW YORK (Fordham)
May 1846–October 1849

RICHMOND (Home of Hugh Pleasants, Tenth and Clay Streets)
Late July 1848–early September 1848

RICHMOND (American Hotel, Eleventh and Main Streets)
July 1849

RICHMOND (Swan Tavern, Eighth and Broad Streets)
July 1849–September 1849

RICHMOND (Madison House, Tenth and Bank Streets)
September 1849

RICHMOND (Duncan Lodge, North Allen and West Broad Streets)
September 1849

BIBLIOGRAPHY

Abugel, Jeffrey. *Edgar Allan Poe's Petersburg: The Untold Story of the Raven in the Cockade City*. Charleston, SC: The History Press, 2013.

Allen, Hervey. *Israfel: The Life and Times of Edgar Allan Poe*. New York: George H. Doren, 1926.

Downey, Christopher Byrd. *Edgar Allan Poe's Charleston*. Charleston, SC: The History Press, 2020.

Harrison, James A. *The Life and Letters of Edgar Allan Poe*. New York: T.Y. Crowell, 1902.

Mabbott, Thomas Ollive. *The Collected Works of Edgar Allan Poe*. Vols. 1–3. Cambridge, MA: Belknap Press of Harvard University Press, 1969 and 1979.

Ocker, J.W. *Poe-Land: The Hallowed Haunts of Edgar Allan Poe*. Woodstock, VT: Countryman Press, 2015.

Ostram, John Ward, Burton Pollin and Jeffrey Savoye. *The Collected Letters of Edgar Allan Poe*. 3rd ed. New York: Gordian Press, 2008.

Phillips, Philip Edward, ed. *Poe and Place*. Cham, Switzerland: Palgrave Macmillan, 2018.

Scott, Mary Wingfield. *Houses of Old Richmond*. New York: Bonanza Books, 1951.

Semtner, Christopher P. *Edgar Allan Poe's Richmond: The Raven in the River City*. Charleston, SC: The History Press, 2012.

———. *The Poe Shrine: Building the World's Finest Edgar Allan Poe Collection*. Charleston, SC: Fonthill Media, 2017.

Silverman, Kenneth. *Edgar Allan Poe: A Mournful and Never-Ending Remembrance*. New York: Harper Perennial, 1992.

Taylor, L.B. *The Ghosts of Virginia*. Vol. 3. Lynchburg, VA: Progress Printing Company, 1996.

Thomas, Dwight, and David K. Jackson. *The Poe Log: A Documentary Life of Edgar Allan Poe, 1809–1849*. Boston: G.K. Hall and Co., 1987.

Weiss, Susan Archer. *The Home Life of Poe*. New York: Broadway Publishing Company, 1907.

ABOUT THE AUTHOR

Visual artist, author and curator of the Edgar Allan Poe Museum in Richmond, Chris Semtner has curated critically acclaimed exhibits for museums and galleries across the country. His publications include the "Poe in Richmond" column for the *Edgar Allan Poe Review*, a biographical introduction to S.S. Van Dine's *The Benson Murder Case*, and chapters for *Edgar Allan Poe in 20 Objects*, *Poe and Place* and *More Than Love: The Enduring Fascination with Edgar Allan Poe*. He has written six books about Poe, visual art and cryptography in addition to contributing articles to Biography.com, Crime Writers' Chronicle and other publications. He has been featured in the *New York Times*, Forbes.com and *Rue Morgue Magazine*, in addition to appearing in documentaries in the United States, the United Kingdom, France, Germany, Spain, Venezuela and Japan. Semtner regularly speaks about strange and macabre subjects at various venues from the Steampunk World's Fair to the Library of Congress and as far away as Japan. Learn more at chrissemtner.com.

Visit us at
www.historypress.com
....